MACAT

T0301946

An Analysis of

Carlo Ginzburg's

The Night Battles
Witchcraft and Agrarian Cults in the 16th anf 17th Centuries

Luke Freeman
with
Etienne Stockland

ROUTLEDGE

Published by Macat International Ltd
24:13 Coda Centre, 189 Munster Road, London SW6 6AW.

Distributed exclusively by Routledge
2 Park Square, Milton Park, Abingdon, Oxon OX14 4RN
711 Third Avenue, New York, NY 10017, USA

Routledge is an imprint of the Taylor & Francis Group, an informa business

www.macat.com
info@macat.com

Cataloguing in Publication Data
A catalogue record for this book is available from the British Library.
Library of Congress Cataloguing-in-Publication Data is available upon request.
Cover illustration: Capucine Deslouis

ISBN 978-1-912302-59-8 (hardback)
ISBN 978-1-912128-86-0 (paperback)
ISBN 978-1-912281-47-3 (e-book)

Notice
The information in this book is designed to orientate readers of the work under analysis,
to elucidate and contextualise its key ideas and themes, and to aid in the development
of critical thinking skills. It is not meant to be used, nor should it be used, as a
substitute for original thinking or in place of original writing or research. References and
notes are provided for informational purposes and their presence does not constitute
endorsement of the information or opinions therein. This book is presented solely for
educational purposes. It is sold on the understanding that the publisher is not engaged
to provide any scholarly advice. The publisher has made every effort to ensure that
this book is accurate and up-to-date, but makes no warranties or representations with
regard to the completeness or reliability of the information it contains. The information
and the opinions provided herein are not guaranteed or warranted to produce particular
results and may not be suitable for students of every ability. The publisher shall not be
liable for any loss, damage or disruption arising from any errors or omissions, or from
the use of this book, including, but not limited to, special, incidental, consequential or
other damages caused, or alleged to have been caused, directly or indirectly, by the
information contained within.

CONTENTS

THE MACAT LIBRARY

The Macat Library is a series of unique academic explorations of seminal works in the humanities and social sciences – books and papers that have had a significant and widely recognised impact on their disciplines. It has been created to serve as much more than just a summary of what lies between the covers of a great book. It illuminates and explores the influences on, ideas of, and impact of that book. Our goal is to offer a learning resource that encourages critical thinking and fosters a better, deeper understanding of important ideas.

Each publication is divided into three Sections: Influences, Ideas, and Impact. Each Section has four Modules. These explore every important facet of the work, and the responses to it.

This Section-Module structure makes a Macat Library book easy to use, but it has another important feature. Because each Macat book is written to the same format, it is possible (and encouraged!) to cross-reference multiple Macat books along the same lines of inquiry or research. This allows the reader to open up interesting interdisciplinary pathways.

To further aid your reading, lists of glossary terms and people mentioned are included at the end of this book (these are indicated by an asterisk [*] throughout) – as well as a list of works cited.

Macat has worked with the University of Cambridge to identify the elements of critical thinking and understand the ways in which six different skills combine to enable effective thinking.
Three allow us to fully understand a problem; three more give us the tools to solve it. Together, these six skills make up the **PACIER** model of critical thinking. They are:

ANALYSIS – understanding how an argument is built
EVALUATION – exploring the strengths and weaknesses of an argument
INTERPRETATION – understanding issues of meaning

CREATIVE THINKING – coming up with new ideas and fresh connections
PROBLEM-SOLVING – producing strong solutions
REASONING – creating strong arguments

To find out more, visit **WWW.MACAT.COM.**

CRITICAL THINKING AND *THE NIGHT BATTLES*

Primary critical thinking skill: CREATIVE THINKING
Secondary critical thinking skill: INTERPRETATION

In *The Night Battles*, Carlo Ginzburg does more than introduce his readers to a novel group of supposed witches – the Benandanti, from the northern Italian province of Friulia. He also invents and deploys new and creative ways of tackling his source material that allow him to move beyond their limitations.

Witchcraft documents are notoriously tricky sources – produced by elites with fixed views, they are products of questioning designed to prove or disprove guilt, rather than understand the subtleties of belief, and are very often the products of torture. Ginzburg placed great stress on variations in the evidence of the Benandanti over time to reveal changing patterns of belief, and also focused on the concept of 'reading against the text' – essentially looking as much at what is absent from the record as at what is present in it, and attempting to understand what the absences mean. His work not only pioneered the creation of a new school of historical study – 'microhistory' – it is also a great example of the creative thinking skills of connecting things together in an original way, producing novel explanations for existing evidence, and redefining an issue so as to see it in a new light.

ABOUT THE AUTHOR OF THE ORIGINAL WORK

Carlo Ginzburg was born in 1939 in the Italian city of Turin during the oppressive regime of dictator Benito Mussolini. His parents, a novelist and a professor of Russian literature, were both active in the anti-fascist movement. As a scholar, Ginzburg went on to found the influential school of 'microhistory,' an approach focusing on very specific events and people as a way to explore and explain a wider social context. He has spent his career teaching in Italy at the universities of Pisa and Bologna, and in the United States at the University of California, Los Angeles.

ABOUT THE AUTHORS OF THE ANALYSIS

Etienne Stockland is researching a PhD in environmental history at Columbia University.

Luke Freeman is a PhD candidate in history at the University of Minnesota, Twin Cities, and teaches as part of the university's 'College in the Schools' program. In addition to his work as an historian, he holds masters degrees in divinity and sacred theology from the Yale University Divinity School.

ABOUT MACAT

GREAT WORKS FOR CRITICAL THINKING

Macat is focused on making the ideas of the world's great thinkers accessible and comprehensible to everybody, everywhere, in ways that promote the development of enhanced critical thinking skills.

It works with leading academics from the world's top universities to produce new analyses that focus on the ideas and the impact of the most influential works ever written across a wide variety of academic disciplines. Each of the works that sit at the heart of its growing library is an enduring example of great thinking. But by setting them in context – and looking at the influences that shaped their authors, as well as the responses they provoked – Macat encourages readers to look at these classics and game-changers with fresh eyes. Readers learn to think, engage and challenge their ideas, rather than simply accepting them.

'Macat offers an amazing first-of-its-kind tool for interdisciplinary learning and research. Its focus on works that transformed their disciplines and its rigorous approach, drawing on the world's leading experts and educational institutions, opens up a world-class education to anyone.'

Andreas Schleicher
Director for Education and Skills, Organisation for Economic Co-operation and Development

'Macat is taking on some of the major challenges in university education ... They have drawn together a strong team of active academics who are producing teaching materials that are novel in the breadth of their approach.'

Prof Lord Broers,
former Vice-Chancellor of the University of Cambridge

'The Macat vision is exceptionally exciting. It focuses upon new modes of learning which analyse and explain seminal texts which have profoundly influenced world thinking and so social and economic development. It promotes the kind of critical thinking which is essential for any society and economy. This is the learning of the future.'

Rt Hon Charles Clarke, former UK Secretary of State for Education

'The Macat analyses provide immediate access to the critical conversation surrounding the books that have shaped their respective discipline, which will make them an invaluable resource to all of those, students and teachers, working in the field.'

Professor William Tronzo, University of California at San Diego

WAYS IN TO THE TEXT

KEY POINTS

- The historian Carlo Ginzburg was born in the Italian city of Turin in 1939 and is particularly noted for his influential work on the Europe of the early-modern* period (roughly the end of the fifteenth century to the end of the eighteenth century).

- *The Night Battles* is a study of men and women of sixteenth- and seventeenth-century Italy who believed they left their bodies at night in the form of animals to battle witches in order to protect their communities.

- In *The Night Battles*, Ginzburg developed an approach to historical research—"microhistory"*—that focuses on specific events, communities, and individuals.

Who is Carlo Ginzburg?

Carlo Ginzburg is an Italian historian noted for his books on sixteenth- and seventeenth-century Europe and for the method of research and analysis he developed to write them—what is known as "microhistory". He was born in the northern Italian city of Turin in 1939. At the time Italy was led by the fascist* dictator Benito Mussolini,* whose regime was characterized by the aggressive suppression of dissent and political opposition.

When Ginzburg was four, his father—the journalist, author, and anti-fascist activist Leone Ginzburg*—was arrested because of his involvement with the newspaper he secretly edited with his wife, Natalia.* Leone died four months later after being tortured in a political prison. A former member of the Communist Party, Natalia went on to have a notable literary career and also entered politics as an independent member of the Italian parliament in 1983.

Carlo Ginzburg gained his PhD at the University of Pisa, where he co-founded *Quaderni Storici* (Historical Notebooks), the journal which was to become the principal mouthpiece of the school of microhistory—an approach to the study of history that focused on very specific events, individuals, and communities. For many years previously, "grand surveys" of nations or societies and the detailed analysis of statistical data had defined the field of history.

A member of the American Philosophical Society and a recipient of the Balzan Prize for an outstanding contribution to the humanities, Ginzburg has spent his career teaching in Italy at the Universities of Pisa and Bologna, and in the United States at the University of California.

He published *The Night Battles* in 1966 and followed it with other papers and books (notably *The Cheese and the Worms,* another highly influential work dealing with Europe of the early-modern period).

What Does *The Night Battles* Say?

The "battles" of the book's title were fought by certain men and women from the Friuli region of north-eastern Italy. At night, Ginzburg writes, these people believed they would leave their bodies and take the shape of animals, such as butterflies and cats, in order to fight witches that threatened their communities. They were known in sixteenth- and seventeenth-century Italy as the *benandanti**—"good walkers."

In *The Night Battles* Ginzburg argues that the *benandanti*'s practices and beliefs were survivals of a pre-Christian cult once followed by farming people across the continent. Indeed, for him their beliefs offer evidence of European shamanism:* a suite of beliefs and rituals that center on the power of a specialist in rituals—the shaman—to enter an altered state of consciousness and to interact with forces "in the world of the spirit" for the benefit of his or her community.

The *benandanti* came to the attention of the Inquisition*—an institution set up by the Roman Catholic Church for the purpose of discovering and punishing heresy,* or violations of Christian doctrine. Although the Inquisition's methods and punishments were notoriously severe, marked by torture and painful execution, it was also a famously bureaucratic institution, keeping detailed records of its trials and punishments. Ginzburg gained access to these records and drew on them to formulate his analysis of who the *benandanti* were, and of their place in European history.

At a time when the study of history was oriented toward *societies* rather than *individuals*, and when researchers tended to focus on educated people of high status, Ginzburg focused on specific men and women of low status. He interpreted their thoughts and deeds with the aim of understanding what they "meant" on their own terms, reading the written sources from the Inquisition for evidence recorded unwittingly, and in spite of their own prejudices and intentions, by their Inquisitors.

This method of analysis—microhistory—was largely developed for *The Night Battles* and has proved to be extremely influential for historians, permanently shifting the focus, assumptions, and aims of historical research and writing.

Why Does *The Night Battles* Matter?
Historical research and analysis have continued to develop since the publication of *The Night Battles* in 1966, and the work's argument on

the nature of European belief has not been without criticism. Yet it remains extremely valuable as a practical demonstration of the microhistorical approach to history. The focus, assumptions, and aims of contemporary historical research owe a great deal to the work of Ginzburg and, in turn, those who have been influenced by it. In consequence, reading *The Night Battles* offers an important view of the context and possibilities of the field today. In addition, the text continues to be important in its own right because of Ginzburg's theoretical and practical innovations.

For the microhistorian, weighty questions can be answered through the study of specific events, communities, and people. Accompanying this idea is the implication that men and women who were not privileged by wealth and status are as valuable to historical research as the highly educated and socially powerful—the people who are frequently considered to be the main drivers of history and the most productive focus of research. According to the microhistorical method, illiterate, powerless, and marginalized people lived lives worthy of study. And to recover their voices is to restore their status as historical actors.

By analyzing written sources against the grain of the intentions and prejudices of the original authors, Ginzburg offered the possibility that illiterate farming people such as the *benandanti* might finally speak for themselves. They could even, perhaps, overcome systems of power that rendered them voiceless.

A similar theoretical approach to analysis saw Ginzburg alter the ways in which historians understood religion, long considered to be a symptom of forces related to economics and social power, or serving a functional role in the life of a community. Ginzburg, however, treated the religious belief of the *benandanti* on its own terms, considering it a component of a world view that might be analyzed as a meaningful historical force in its own right. In this way he paved the way for other influential works of religious history that continued where he left off.

Reading *The Night Battles*, it is difficult to distinguish between the subject and the methodological approach. We might be obliged to consider what might be gained from changing our attitude to the sources available to us, and what might be gained from shifting our focus to overlooked and apparently incidental evidence in those sources. We might even have to reconsider the very nature of a useful source.

SECTION 1
INFLUENCES

MODULE 1
THE AUTHOR AND THE
HISTORICAL CONTEXT

KEY POINTS

- *The Night Battles* is a foundational work of microhistory,*
  a school of historical research and writing developed in the
  1960s.

- Along with the Italian historians Giovanni Levi* and
  Carlo Poni*, Carlo Ginzburg founded a journal, *Quaderni
  Storici*, which became the main organ for the school of
  microhistory.

- 1960s Marxist* readings of history favored the structural
  sociology* view that culture must be considered in the
  light of larger structures that define societies—particularly
  economics and class. Microhistory emerged as an
  alternative to this view.

Why Read This Text?

Published in 1966, Carlo Ginzburg's *The Night Battles: Witchcraft and
Agrarian Cults in the Sixteenth and Seventeenth Centuries* was an essential
text in the founding of the intellectual school that was to become
known as microhistory.

Microhistory was developed largely in response to the research and
writing of the *Annales** historians—an intellectual school, dominant
in historical research since the 1930s, and associated with the French
academic journal *Annales d'Histoire Economique et Sociale* (Annals of
Economic and Social History). *Annales* historians such as Fernand
Braudel,* sought to write total history,* or macrohistory,* through
the analysis of large-scale geographical, economic, demographic, and
social structures.[1]

> ❝ Microhistory is a form of historical analysis and writing, a genre. It takes a single, focused, historical 'moment' and uses it to shine light on a broader world. ❞
> Steven Bednarski, *A Poisoned Past: The Life and Times of Margarida De Portu, A Fourteenth-Century Accused Poisoner*

This structuralist* approach minimized the importance both of individuals and events, favoring instead analyses of the ways in which social structures determined history. Many historians, however, were dissatisfied with the methods and assumptions of the *Annales* school. Microhistorians such as Ginzburg tested those methods and assumptions by turning to sources that reflected the beliefs, hopes, and lives of *individuals*.

The subject of Ginzburg's *The Night Battles* was a group of people from north-eastern Italy known as the *benandanti*,* or "good walkers," a loose affiliation of peasants who believed they left their bodies at night and fought battles with malevolent forces to protect their crops. Members of the *benandanti* were tried for witchcraft by the Inquisition*—an institution set up by the Roman Catholic Church* to investigate and punish heresy* (beliefs that went against traditional Christian ideas).

In discussing this notable corner of Italian history, Ginzburg focused on individuals among the *benandanti* and their beliefs—areas of inquiry that the total history of the *Annales* school would not have considered.

Author's Life

Carlo Ginzburg was born in 1939 in the Italian city of Turin to parents with left-leaning, communist* politics. His mother, Natalia,* was a novelist. His father, Leone,* was a professor of Russian literature in the city of Pisa and a specialist on the Russian intellectual Mikhail Bakhtin.* An anti-fascist* activist, Leone died in a political prison under the regime of the fascist dictator Benito Mussolini* in 1944.

Political analysis is not an important feature of *The Night Battles*. However, given that his father was persecuted for his political beliefs, and ultimately died while a political prisoner, it seems possible that Ginzburg's family history may have provoked his interest in persecuted and marginal groups like the *benandanti*. As Ginzburg himself recalled 40 years after the initial 1966 publication of *The Night Battles*: "Only much later did I understand my emotional identification, as a Jew,* with victims of the Inquisition, and later still my intellectual contact with the Inquisitors."[2]

The Night Battles was originally published in Italy while Ginzburg was a professor at the University of Pisa. He studied under Delio Cantimori,* a scholar of the turbulent period in European religious history known as the Reformation,* whose interests in heretical beliefs and practices were surely an influence on Ginzburg's career.

At Pisa, Ginzburg helped found the school of microhistory with the Italian scholars Giovanni Levi and Carlo Poni.[3] These historians published their works in *Quaderni Storici* (Historical Notebooks), a journal Ginzburg co-founded and which became the principal mouthpiece of the microhistorical school. Indeed, *Quaderni Storici* became a rival to the French *Annales*—the highly influential journal of the macrohistorical school of total history.

Author's Background

The Night Battles was published at a time when orthodox Marxist histories were under scrutiny. Dissatisfaction with Marxist methodology stemmed, in part, from concerns over the use of modern economic categories such as "working class" in the analysis of societies that existed before industrialization.* In the traditional Marxist view of history, individuals did not shape their own destinies and desires. Rather, their lives were simply reflections of larger historical forces that dictated the unrelenting rise of the working class. As a result, the reaction to total history was underpinned by both political and methodological concerns.

Marxist historians focused on large groups of people as a point of methodology. Ginzburg, on the other hand, while politically influenced by Marxism, challenged the methodological focus of Marxist historians, centering his inquiry on individuals or small social groups, such as the *benandanti*.

Ginzburg also challenged the Marxist idea that social structures hold sway over the freedom of individuals, by analyzing how individuals made choices both within social structures and at their margins.

At the time of the publication of *The Night Battles*, the Marxist-influenced *Annales* school was dominant in Italy. Members of the school minimized the importance of individuals and events, and instead favored analyses of demographic, social, and economic structures. Microhistorians, by contrast, responded by going to sources that reflected the beliefs, hopes, and lives of individuals.

To better explain how Ginzburg differed from the *Annales* historians, it might be useful to compare nuclear physicists and astronomical physicists. Both seek to understand how the universe works. While the astronomer finds evidence through data gathered from the "macro" world of space and billions of stars and galaxies, the nuclear physicist looks at the "micro" world of the atom.

NOTES

1   David A. Bell, "Total History and Microhistory: The French and Italian Paradigms," in *A Companion to Western Historical Thought*, ed. Lloyd Kramer and Sarah Maza (Oxford: Blackwell, 2002), 262–76.

2   Carlo Ginzburg, "Preface to the 2013 edition," *The Night Battles: Witchcraft and Agrarian Cults in the Sixteenth and Seventeenth Centuries*, trans. John and Anne C. Tedeschi (Baltimore, MD: Johns Hopkins University Press, 2013), x.

3   Carlo Ginzburg, "Microhistory: Two or Three Things That I Know About It," trans. John and Anne C. Tedeschi, *Critical Inquiry* 20, no. 1 (1993): 10–35.

MODULE 2
ACADEMIC CONTEXT

KEY POINTS

- Social historians* (historians interested in the dynamics of social groups rather than individuals) seek to provide a view of history "from below"—from the vantage point of those often sidelined by traditional histories.

- Until the 1960s, the field of social history was dominated by Marxist* historians.

- Carlo Ginzburg's microhistorical* approach sought to understand popular culture and belief systems.

The Work in Its Context

While Carlo Ginzburg was researching and writing *The Night Battles*, social historians in Europe were increasingly curious about the ways in which masses of people changed over time; Marxist historians were particularly interested in taking the laboring, lower classes as their main object of study. Although Ginzburg was similarly influenced by the possibility of writing history from the perspective of people at the bottom of society, *The Night Battles* was primarily concerned with popular culture and belief.

Ginzburg was drawn to the examination of the collective psychology of individuals rather than to the analysis of grand cultural and social structures, He developed the microhistorical method with the aim of mining historical minutiae—that is, tiny pieces of information and "insignificant details"—for evidence of larger intellectual and cultural trends.

As the American historian Brad Gregory* has remarked, the turn toward historical methods on the micro scale reflected broader

> **❝** The most fruitful contribution of the social historians has been to focus the spotlight on groups that have typically been ignored in traditional history—women, racial and ethnic minorities, blue-collar and migrant workers, farmers, peasants, children, the aged, criminals, outcasts, and groups otherwise marginalized by society. **❞**
>
> Conal Furay and Michael J. Salevouris, *The Methods and Skills of History: A Practical Guide*

currents of thought among the intellectual left* in the period after World War II.* In the 1970s, faith in the ability to liberate "humanity through the transformation of industrial capitalism* became increasingly untenable."[1] So social historians turned to the study of the details of everyday life with the aim of shedding light on the actions of individuals and on the development of large, seemingly impersonal structural forces—capitalism, for example—that touched the lives of those individuals.

By specifically focusing on the experiences of individuals, microhistorians were seeking to understand the past, both politically and culturally, while avoiding the traditional Marxist interpretation that the progress of history was decided by modes of production. This was called the "determinist"* assumption of traditional Marxist historical analysis.

Overview of the Field

In the period when Ginzburg wrote *The Night Battles*, French historians and thinkers, most notably the *Annales* school, were particularly influential in Italy. The journal's founders, Marc Bloch,* Lucien Febvre,* and Fernand Braudel,* were trying to create total history*—an account of the past that drew on quantifiable data such as grain prices and the size of land holdings to understand large structural transformations over long periods of time.[2]

This approach, however, tended to conceal the role of individual action in the making of history and to assume, by and large, that culture and ideas were the effects of other, greater, forces and social structures. Indeed, in Fernand Braudel's totalistic vision of history, the lives of individuals were like "crests of foam that the tides of history carry on their strong back."[3]

While it is true that in the 1950s and 1960s some historians within the *Annales* school advocated a turn toward the study of attitudes, ideas, and culture, labeling it *histoire des mentalités*[4] (the history of mentalities*), these historians remained wedded to the quantitative* social scientific methods that were the mark of the *Annales* thinking. This meant they were still particularly concerned with the interpretation of statistical data. Microhistory emerged, as the historian David Bell* remarks, out of a "methodological disillusionment with quantitative social science."[5]

The tendencies of the *Annales* school provided Ginzburg with an intellectual basis for his historical theory. Microhistory—as Ginzburg and his colleague Carlo Poni* declared in 1979—was a "newly successful Italian export that had managed to upset a pattern of French–Italian intellectual trade long weighted in favor of France."[6]

Academic Influences

In *The Night Battles*, Ginzburg argues that an ancient agrarian cult stretching throughout European farmlands had survived up to the seventeenth century. However, he could not have formulated this argument were it not for the method developed by the French anthropologist Claude Lévi-Strauss* (1908–2009) and the Russian folklorist and scholar Vladimir Propp* (1895–1970). As Ginzburg later recalled, the non-ethnocentric* approach he adopted in *The Night Battles* arrived in large part through "comparison with the work of anthropologists, first among whom was Claude Lévi-Strauss."[7]

Lévi-Strauss's work gave Ginzburg the idea that individual choices are curtailed by social structures; from there he turned to the margins of social structures to consider the small adjustments and choices made by individuals. Propp, meanwhile, offered Ginzburg a means to compare apparently similar practices and beliefs separated by time and space in order to analyze them. By drawing on the disciplinary concerns of history and anthropology, Ginzburg pushed the boundaries of both, helping to create a field known as historical anthropology.*

The scholarly concern for the minutiae—that is, the smaller details—of everyday life itself can be traced back to the works of the sociologist Georg Simmel* (1858–1918), the philosopher Walter Benjamin* (1892–1940), and the theorist Siegfried Kracauer* (1889–1966). All of these German authors were cited by Ginzburg as an "indirect influence" on his work.[8] Yet for Ginzburg, as for all these writers, a turn toward detail was not an end in itself. It had a political function—to open history, as the historians Edward Muir and Guido Ruggiero have remarked, "to peoples who would be left out by other methods."[9]

These "peoples" were historical figures, both individuals and groups, neglected in accounts of the past because of their status or marginal nature. Ginzburg followed the call of the Marxist historian E. P. Thompson* to rescue them from the "enormous condescension of posterity"[10] by acknowledging their historical importance and by writing history "from below."

NOTES

1   Brad S. Gregory, "Is Small Beautiful? Microhistory and the History of Everyday Life," *History and Theory* 38, no. 1 (1999): 101.

2   Peter Burke, *The French Historical Revolution: The Annales School, 1929–1989* (Cambridge: Polity Press, 1990).

3   Fernand Braudel, *The Mediterranean and the Mediterranean World in the Age of Philip II* (New York: Harper and Row, 1972), 20–1.

4   Philippe Ariès, "L'Histoire des mentalités," in *La Nouvelle Histoire*, ed. Jacques Legoff, Roger Chartier, and Jacques Revel (Paris: Retz-CEPL, 1978), 411.

5   David A. Bell, "Total History and Microhistory: The French and Italian Paradigms," in *A Companion to Western Historical Thought*, ed. Lloyd Kramer and Sarah Maza (Oxford: Blackwell, 2002), 266.

6   Bell, "Total History and Microhistory," 270.

7   Carlo Ginzburg, "Microhistory: Two or Three Things That I Know About It," trans. John and Anne C. Tedeschi, *Critical Inquiry* 20, no. 1 (1993): 22.

8   John Brewer, "Microhistory and the Histories of Everyday Life," *Cultural and Social History* 7, no. 1 (2010): 99.

9   Edward Muir and Guido Ruggiero, eds., *Microhistory and the Lost Peoples of Europe* (Baltimore, MD: Johns Hopkins University Press, 1991), xxi.

10 E. P. Thompson, *The Making of the English Working Class* (London: Victor Gollancz, 1963), 12–13.

MODULE 3
THE PROBLEM

KEY POINTS

- For the most part, historians of witchcraft in the 1960s and 1970s looked to society in their attempts explain the witch hunts* that took place in Europe between the fifteenth and eighteenth centuries.

- The dominant framework for explaining belief in witchcraft was the structural-functionalist* approach.

- Carlo Ginzburg's microsocial* approach, inspired partly by the work of the American anthropologist Clifford Geertz,* sought to reconstruct understanding of belief systems by thinking about the ways in which individuals expressed their beliefs in their social context.

Core Question

The 1960s saw an increased interest in early-modern* witchcraft and heretical* belief (opinions that were at odds with those of the Church). Carlo Ginzburg's mentor and advisor, the historian Delio Cantimori,* had built a successful and influential career on researching beliefs and practices considered to be heretical.

At the time *The Night Battles* was published in 1966, historians of witchcraft were primarily interested in developing sociological explanations for the witch hunts and "witch crazes" of the sixteenth and seventeenth centuries[1] in which people believed to be witches were persecuted, the practice often being stoked by a sense of moral outrage and general hysteria. Witch hunts took place in Europe in the early-modern period, and as many as 100,000 people were killed. These historians were more interested in *societies* than *individuals*.

> ❝ I have become convinced that many of the insights of the social anthropologist can be profitably applied to the study of history, and that is nowhere more so than in the case of the history of witchcraft—a topic which most historians regard as peripheral, not to say bizarre, but which has always been central to the British anthropological tradition. ❞
>
> Keith Thomas, "The Relevance of Social Anthropology to the Historical Study of English Witchcraft"

Furthermore, the attention given to witchcraft beliefs tended to focus solely on educated people of high status.[2]

In this context, Ginzburg opted for a radical move. He attempted to interpret the beliefs and daily practices of peasant religion, particularly witchcraft, in order to understand what this ideology meant for the individuals who adhered to it. Ginzburg's research was founded on the assumption that answers can be constructed "from below"—that is, by considering the thought and social context of people of lower status without relying on the terminology and categories of the historically powerful, such as the Inquisitors, who were tasked by the Roman Catholic Church* to investigate and punish heresy.*

The subject of *The Night Battles*, then, was the beliefs and practices of the *benandanti*,* a loose affiliation of sixteenth- and seventeenth-century peasants who believed they left their bodies at night to defend their crops and communities from attacks by evil spiritual forces (often called *maldandanti*—"bad walkers"). Ginzburg assumed that the *benandanti* could still speak for themselves, using their own words to express their ideas and beliefs—even through the transcripts of the hostile, partial Inquisitorial trials they were forced to suffer.

The Participants

In the 1960s, the study of early-modern witchcraft was dominated by the structural-functionalist school of interpretation.[3] According to this view, witchcraft and witchcraft accusations performed certain social functions—helping people cope with stress and fear, for example, or with unexplainable traumas such as illness and death.

The structural-functionalist approach was first advocated by the British historian Hugh Trevor-Roper,* whose book *The European Witch-Craze of the Sixteenth and Seventeenth Centuries* marked the beginning of an attempt to apply structural sociology* to the study of European witchcraft.

Another exponent of the functionalist* interpretation was the British social historian Keith Thomas,* author of a key study of magical beliefs and practices in sixteenth- and seventeenth century England, *Religion and the Decline of Magic.* The "decline" in those magical beliefs and practices, he theorized, was caused by the rise of medical science. Practitioners of magic, he believed, had played a similar social function to modern doctors.

Followers of the functionalist school of interpretation made little attempt to understand popular beliefs in witchcraft on their own terms. Indeed, Hugh Trevor-Roper discouraged historians from inquiring into the meaning of witch belief. In a book examining religion and social change, he went so far as to describe belief in witchcraft as "the mental rubbish of peasant credulity and feminine hysteria."[4]

In this context, Ginzburg's study of witchcraft was quite distinctive. His inquiry led him to analyze the *meaning* of witchcraft at a time when other scholars were principally concerned with its function in society.

The Contemporary Debate

Ginzburg's approach to the study of witchcraft was at odds with that of other contemporary scholars. The dominant trend in the field followed the work of Keith Thomas and the British anthropologist and historian Alan Macfarlane,* researchers and thinkers who had drawn on the structuralist social anthropology of E. E. Evans-Pritchard* to explain the rise and fall of witchcraft beliefs.[5]

Ginzburg's work aligned him with anthropologists such as Clifford Geertz, whose method of "thick description" has much in common with the method of microscopic analysis employed in *The Night Battles.* Thick description is the idea that minute observations can be made understandable if they are related to the social context in which they belong. *The Night Battles* exemplifies this approach: First the testimony of the *benandanti* is studied for the microscopic details; then the minute decisions revealed in such testimony are fitted into a large-scale system of meaning.

By the 1980s the Macfarlane–Thomas model was being ousted from its central place in the historical study of witchcraft by the new Geertzian anthropological approach developed by Ginzburg and other scholars. In this period, as the British historian Malcolm Gaskill writes, "critics of Macfarlane and Thomas objected that their pre-war functionalist anthropology seemed rather stale, especially in the post-colonial era when witchcraft and witch-hunting were acquiring new significance."[6]

Since the 1990s, the dominant trend in research into witchcraft has been to recover the meaning and experience of witchcraft *within* the cultural and intellectual framework of specific groups.[7] These culturally oriented histories of witchcraft owe a great deal to the pioneering methods developed by Ginzburg in the *The Night Battles.*

NOTES

1   Marijke Giswijt-Hofstra, "The European Witchcraft Debate and the Dutch Variant," *Social History* 15, no. 2 (1990): 181–94.

2   As evidenced by the essays in Sydney Anglo, ed., *The Damned Art: Essays in the Literature of Witchcraft* (London, Henley, and Boston: Routledge & Kegan Paul, 1977).

3   E. William Monter, "The Historiography of European Witchcraft: Progress and Prospects," *Journal of Interdisciplinary History* 2, no. 4 (1972): 435–53.

4   H. R. Trevor-Roper, *Religion, the Reformation, and Social Change*, 2nd edn. (London: Macmillan, 1972), 116.

5   Alan Macfarlane, *Witchcraft in Tudor and Stuart England: A Regional and Comparative Study* (London: Routledge & Kegan Paul, 1970); Keith Thomas, *Religion and the Decline of Magic* (New York: C. Scribner's Sons, 1971).

6   Malcolm Gaskill, "The Pursuit of Reality: Recent Research into the History of Witchcraft," *The Historical Journal* 51, no. 4 (2008): 1071.

7   Gaskill, "Pursuit of Reality," 1069–88.

MODULE 4
THE AUTHOR'S CONTRIBUTION

KEY POINTS

- Carlo Ginzburg's aim was to reconstruct the mental worlds of men and women accused of witchcraft in sixteenth- and seventeenth-century Italy.

- His microhistorical* approach was welcomed at a time when the assumption that history might be understood through the analysis of statistical data—the serial history* approach—was falling out of favor.

- Ginzburg believed that it was possible to study the mentalities* of ordinary people to better understand the world and society they lived in.

Author's Aims

In *The Night Battles*, Carlo Ginzburg argues for the existence of a Europe-wide pre-Christian* fertility cult* that had survived into the sixteenth century. This fertility cult, he says, informed the behavior of a group of peasants from north-eastern Italy known as the *benandanti.** Ginzburg tried to write this history "from below"—that is, from the perspective of poor or marginalized individuals, paying particular attention to the thoughts, actions, and beliefs of people long forgotten.

While Marxist* historians were, by and large, interested in the development of social classes that we might be able to identify today, Ginzburg focused on people who have disappeared from history and society. People with magical and heretical* beliefs were ideally suited for his research.

In the 1960s, when historical research was driven by the analysis of large quantities of statistical data, Ginzburg's intention was to secure a

66 The contrast between the crude models of elite vs. popular culture in the historiography of the 1970s and Bourdieu-influenced models of cultural fluidity and adaptability of the 1990s could not be more stark. The works of ... Carlo Ginzburg and other pioneers have essentially rendered unutilizable much of the scholarship about 'popular culture' written in the 1970s and even in the 1980s. 99

James B. Collins and Karen L. Taylor, "Research Paradigms, Old and New" in *Early Modern Europe: Issues and Interpretations*

place in history for *individuals*. The emotions, ideas, and hopes that make individuals what they are, he claimed, are available to historical study, and can be helpful in understanding change over time. This approach was in stark contrast to serial history's data-driven approach to social history advocated by historians such as the Frenchman François Furet.*

Ginzburg took particular exception to Furet's claim that "the history of subaltern [that is, lower-status] classes in preindustrial societies can only be studied from a statistical point of view."[1] Ginzburg believed his method of historical research did not adequately account for the actions of individual historical figures. Rejecting Furet's view led Ginzburg to develop an approach that focused on the minute analysis of specific events involving otherwise ignored historical actors or groups.

Approach

The methodology Ginzburg adopts provides *The Night Battles* with a coherent plan. First, he establishes the historical events surrounding the Inquisitorial* trials of the individuals he aims to analyze: the *benandanti*. He then shows how the Inquisitors misunderstood the accused. Once he has separated the reader's understanding of the *benandanti* from the accounts of the Inquisitors, he searches out parallel groups in historical records, establishing a new understanding of the *benandanti* that casts them as part of an ancient agricultural cult.

Ginzburg's analysis continues by discussing why it might have been that the *benandanti* themselves came to reject this self-definition and to accept the Inquisitors' perception of them as heretical witches involved in satanic worship.

When Ginzburg wrote *The Night Battles*, the Vatican's* official Inquisition Archives were not open to all researchers, and Ginzburg limited his research to regional records held in local archives outside Rome. He did not, however, simply take these court documents at face value. Mistrusting the way the Inquisitors chose to see the people on trial, Ginzburg instead attempted to understand the minds of the accused in their own terms.

For him, popular beliefs outside of orthodox Christian doctrine, including witchcraft, should be understood as structurally distinct from, or even opposed to, that orthodox doctrine. According to Ginzburg's analysis, a tradition of agrarian customs that were older than Christianity had survived until the sixteenth century.

Contribution in Context

When *The Night Battles* was first published in 1966, the field of history was characterized by research that relied on collections of statistical data. In an effort to write total history,* many publications were based on such matters as death rates, birth rates, crop yields, and so on—a question of *quantities* rather than *qualities*. In France, where this statistical approach was particularly dominant, only the historian Emmanuel Le Roy Ladurie* looked to address *qualities*, reconstructing the social and cultural worlds of specifically defined groups.

Ginzburg's research into the mental world inhabited by individuals implicitly suggests two things about historical research. The first is that the individual mind can be considered a reflection of the changes experienced by the world and society, and that this reflection is both practical and useful to the researcher. The second is perhaps more significant and audacious. It is an implicit understanding that the mentality and motives of past individuals are available to the historian.

The first notion positioned Ginzburg outside the mainstream of historical research, while the second placed him outside the mainstream of the field of social studies more generally—a field where real skepticism about our ability to understand the minds of other people dominated.

NOTES

1   Carlo Ginzburg, "Microhistory: Two or Three Things That I Know About It," trans. John and Anne C. Tedeschi, *Critical Inquiry* 20, no. 1 (1993): 22.

SECTION 2
IDEAS

MODULE 5
MAIN IDEAS

KEY POINTS

- The central theme of Carlo Ginzburg's text is the opposition between elite and popular culture.

- In *The Night Battles*, Ginzburg argued that it was the Inquisitors'* preconceived view of the benandanti* that led to the latter group eventually agreeing that they were witches.

- Ginzburg wanted his book to appeal both to specialists and to a wider audience.

Key Themes

Carlo Ginzburg's *The Night Battles* investigates the *benandanti*, or "good walkers," a loose affiliation of sixteenth-century peasants in northern Italy who claimed to be protecting local crops by having night-time battles with spiritual forces.

While the work focuses on a small collection of individuals and their beliefs, *The Night Battles* puts forward the idea that there was, in fact, a pan-European, pre-Christian rural cult. Ginzburg relies on anthropological methods to identify the *benandanti*'s various practices and beliefs. Once identified, he then interprets them in the light of similarities to other European beliefs, notably the "witches' sabbath"*—a ritual involving, among other things, the perversion of Roman Catholic symbols—and the idea that people could transform into wolves or other animals. By comparing the *benandanti*'s beliefs and practices to other local beliefs and practices dating back to the pre-Christian era, Ginzburg is able to greatly widen the scope of his historical interpretation.

" In this book I have studied the religious attitudes and, in a broad sense, the mentality of a peasant society—the Friulian—between the end of the sixteenth century and the first half of the seventeenth, but from an extremely limited point of view; the history of a nucleus of popular beliefs, which little by little, as a result of specific forces, became assimilated by witchcraft. It is an episode in history that has been unknown until now, but one which casts a great deal of light on the general problem of witchcraft and its persecution. "

Carlo Ginzburg, preface to the Italian edition of *The Night Battles*

The Night Battles is also concerned with demonstrating how these popular belief systems were understood by groups of people of high social standing. A significant proportion of the book stresses the inability of the Inquisition to understand who the *benandanti* really were. As Ginzburg demonstrates, the Inquisitors' expectations were shaped by their concept of witchcraft. As a consequence, they eventually came to see the *benandanti* as witches, rather than as innocents. Importantly for Ginzburg's account, they did so without ever truly understanding the *benandanti's* practices and beliefs.

Ginzburg's first task, then, was to lay bare the Inquisitors' failure to properly comprehend and describe the *benandanti*, and afterwards to attempt to recover what they, as a group, might have been.

Exploring the Ideas

In its exploration of the competition between popular and elite belief systems, *The Night Battles* stresses the historical importance of social imbalances of power.

Ginzburg describes a process by which the socially powerful (in this case, the Inquisitors) are allowed to determine the meaning of the practices of those less socially powerful (in this case, the *benandanti*). He shows how the *benandanti*, when first investigated by the Inquisitors, were convinced that they were not witches and that the Inquisitors themselves shared this opinion, despite their general confusion about what the *benandanti* were really up to.

Tracing the *benandanti*'s progression from innocence to guilt in the eyes of the Inquisition, Ginzburg suggests that some of the misunderstanding lay in linguistic confusion. The *benandanti* spoke a regional dialect of northern Italy called "Friulian," which the Inquisitors did not. However, this was only a practical difficulty, and Ginzburg is much more interested in the false impressions that arose due to the expectations and preconceptions the Inquisitors brought with them.

By structuring his analysis around the theme of inequality, Ginzburg is able to free the *benandanti* from the Inquisition's verdict (even if they themselves eventually agreed with it) and then to investigate more fully who the *benandanti* really were.

Language and Expression

"The present book," wrote Ginzburg in the preface to *The Night Battles*, "was not written only for specialists. Without sacrificing scholarly rigor, I hoped to reach a wider audience."

The "specialists" in question were historians interested in the ways in which popular beliefs developed and changed over time, and anthropologists interested in forms of interaction between and across urban elite cultures and popular rural cultures. Although *The Night Battles* has shaped the studies of historians *and* anthropologists, the work's gripping narrative allowed Ginzburg to reach the "wider audience" he hoped for.[1]

The Night Battles offers explanations of the workings of popular belief in rural Italy and the ways in which these beliefs relate to elite and urban structures. Although the work did not give rise to any particular term or concept, Ginzburg's methodology proved to be significantly influential for those researching and writing on the social history of popular beliefs.

As the historian John Martin remarked in the early 1990s: "Recently … the fashionableness of the study of the popular culture of the early-modern* period has created a climate in which it has become possible to attempt a history of the beliefs that underlay notions of popular witchcraft and magic … It is to Carlo Ginzburg's credit to have made several rich suggestions about ways around these and similar obstacles."[2]

The attempt to read documents produced by people of high status in order to excavate and interpret marginalized popular belief systems became the hallmark of a generation of social historians who embraced microhistory.*

NOTES

1 Carlo Ginzburg, "Preface to the Italian Edition," *The Night Battles: Witchcraft and Agrarian Cults in the Sixteenth and Seventeenth Centuries*, trans. John and Anne C. Tedeschi, (Baltimore, MD: Johns Hopkins University Press, 2013), xii.

2 John Martin, "Journeys to the World of the Dead: The Work of Carlo Ginzburg," *Journal of Social History* 25, no. 3 (1992): 613.

MODULE 6
SECONDARY IDEAS

KEY POINTS

- Carlo Ginzburg's text sought to illuminate the ways in which a historical record is shaped by geographical and social forces.

- The practice of reading sources to uncover insights that were not intentionally recorded by the writers of those sources has become a useful tool in the study of social history.

- Recently, Ginzburg's findings have led to interpretations of witchcraft that pay special attention to issues associated with gender.

Other Ideas

One of the key secondary ideas in Carlo Ginzburg's *The Night Battles* is the way in which the historian's craft is shaped by the nature of the available sources. Ginzburg explores this by considering the relationship between geography and the historical record; the small size of Italy's regions, he notes, impedes the historian's ability to make sweeping conclusions about large geographical areas.

As Ginzburg argues in an essay in the book *Microhistory* and the Lost Peoples of Europe*, Italy's geography, with its valleys, mountainous dead ends, and long coastlines, distinguishes it from countries like France, which are characterized by large, semi-continuous regions. If geographic circumstances influence the type of sources available to Italian historians, Ginzurg writes, then Italian history should reflect that.[2]

The Night Battles also contributed to larger questions about the ways in which social power is reflected in the historical record.

66 In the forty years since Carlo Ginzburg surprised historians with evidence that a set of archaic beliefs about supernatural nocturnal battles waged by specially endowed people was flourishing in Italy's northeastern corner in the late sixteenth century, subsequent research has enormously extended our information about their shamanistic analogs into widely scattered corners of the European world and far beyond ... Forty years ago, it is not surprising that the idea of separating the *benandanti* into men and women seems not to have occurred to Ginzburg, although his earliest examples were men, while some later examples were women.[1] 99

E. William Monter, "Gendering the Extended Family of Ginzburg's Benandanti"

Significantly, the book's arguments are based on the assumption that sources produced by the socially powerful both clarify *and* obscure historical events: according to Ginzburg, those with high status generally over-theorize events, while the less privileged tend to keep meaning closer to everyday experience itself.

In *The Night Battles*, this assumption is reflected in the Inquisitors'* desire to apply witch-theory to the practices of the *benandanti*.* The *benandanti* themselves, for whom theory was not practically relevant, took the meaning of their practices to be self-evident.

Ginzburg's implication is that to take sources written by those of elite status at face value means perpetuating elite social power over historians and the historically voiceless alike.

Exploring the Ideas

While Ginzburg laid out some of the ways that documentary records have shaped historical writing, he did not believe these constraints were definitive. He did not accept, for example, that Italy's geography limited the general conclusions that could be made by research into Italian history.

Ginzburg proposes that sources may be uncovered through microscopic analysis, but that does not mean that historical conclusions should also be small in scope. To prove it, he makes large-scale claims about the ways people relate to one another and to their environment.

Moreover, Ginzburg believed that the prejudices of the powerful people who tended to shape the documentary record could be overcome if their writings were assessed critically. Indeed, in *The Night Battles*, Ginzburg proceeds on the assumption that a historian can know a subject more intimately and accurately than contemporary witnesses. This can be seen in his rejection of the Inquisitors' judgment of the *benandanti* and in the understanding he proposes to replace it. As a result, the book insists on certain claims about the nature of sources and the relationship of historians to the subject of their inquiry.

Overlooked

The most overlooked aspect of *The Night Battles* concerns gender. Beginning in 1581, investigations into the *benandanti* predominantly involved men. Later Inquisitorial activity, ending in 1670, focused almost exclusively on women.

The American historian E. William Monter* recently attempted to reframe Ginzburg's account as part of a larger discussion about the relationships between gender, magical healing, and witchcraft.[3] Monter finds that European men often feature in accounts of magical healers—a practice undertaken by some of the *benandanti* described by Ginzburg. Monter's suggestion is that the *benandanti*'s shamanistic* ritual practices, of which magical healing was a crucial component, might be as strongly connected to contemporary notions of gender as they are to conceptions of magic. In other words, historical research into persecutions of witches might begin by first analyzing the relationship between gender and witchcraft. It might continue by asking if being a male witch (or shaman) meant the same thing as being a female witch. Monter suggests that the meaning was not shared across Europe's various regions.

Given that Ginzburg's research carefully notes the gender of each accused *benandante*, his text is relevant in discussions about the different ways male and female witches were treated. If today it seems odd that Ginzburg's text does not deal more explicitly with gender, it is worthwhile remembering that he scrupulously avoids introducing interpretive modes (that is, "ways in" useful to ground and expand some way of making sense of the material) that are not present in the sources themselves. So if the Inquisitors and the *benandanti* did not refer to gender themselves, then reading it back into the sources would introduce modern conceptions of gender. Regardless of Ginzburg's method, however, there is evidence that male and female witches were treated differently across late medieval* and early-modern* Europe.

The changes in the *benandanti*'s descriptions of themselves range from "heretical* but Catholic*" to "practitioners of witchcraft." These changes run parallel to the Inquisitors' shifting focus from men to women, and it is worth looking to *The Night Battles* for a contribution to the larger inquiry into pan-European conceptions of gender, and religious and cult spiritual practice.

As Monter notes, Ginzburg's *The Night Battles* has provided the point of departure for more "sharply focused empirical investigations in order to obtain a clearer notion of exactly where and how mainly (but not exclusively) male shamans impact the still-understudied gendering of two closely related fields, witchcraft accusations and magical healing."[4]

NOTES

1   E. William Monter, "Gendering the Extended Family of Ginzburg's Benandanti," *Magic, Ritual, and Witchcraft* 1, no. 2 (2006): 222, 224.

2   Carlo Ginzburg and Carlo Poni, "The Name and the Game: Unequal Exchange and the Historiographic Marketplace," in *Microhistory and the Lost Peoples of Europe*, ed. Edward Muir and Guido Ruggiero (Baltimore, MD: Johns Hopkins University Press, 1991), 1–10.

3   Monter, "Gendering."

4   Monter, "Gendering," 226.

MODULE 7
ACHIEVEMENT

KEY POINTS

- Carlo Ginzburg's *The Night Battles* helped establish microhistory* as a central tool for social historians.*

- *The Night Battles* was published at a time of heightened interest in the thoughts of people outside the elite.

- Ginzburg's *The Night Battles* was criticized for "reaching" to make conclusions not supported by the limited evidence it presented.

Assessing the Argument

Carlo Ginzburg's *The Night Battles* helped establish the techniques of microhistory as central to the practice of social historians. The book presented a different viewpoint from the mid-twentieth-century method of researching and writing total history,* a school uninterested in analyzing events or individuals, favoring instead the writing of history according to economic, demographic, and social investigations. For those who believed in total history, events or individuals were simply reflections of larger historical forces and did not affect historical outcomes. Ginzburg and microhistory challenged historians—especially those writing total history—to reflect on how successfully their accounts aligned with the experience of those who actually "lived" history.

The influence of *The Night Battles* can be seen in the growth of microhistory in the years immediately after its publication in Italy in 1966 and, in English translation, in 1983. In both cases, the book furthered social history (the study of society and social structures) and cultural history* (the study of the development of culture). As the

> ❝ Ginzburg's historiographical exploitation of these gaps, his extraordinary ability to read the codes, furnishes evidence for a set of phenomena that gives us a *more accurate* characterization of the *benandanti*.* Whatever the distortions of the Inquisitorial evidence, Ginzburg's procedure of reading the gaps does culminate in genuine evidence about a cultural reality that is no longer inaccessible to us. ❞
>
> Arnold I. Davidson, *The Emergence of Sexuality: Historical Epistemology and the Formation of Concepts*

social historian István Szijártó* has recently remarked, microhistory is today "the flagship of contemporary social historians, taking over from historical anthropology,* and being intertwined with new cultural history."[1]

Achievement in Context

Ginzburg's text emerged at a time of heightened interest in the study of popular mentalities*—the "mindset" of people not necessarily privileged with economic and social power. It was published at a time of growing disenchantment with the method of writing history that made use of large amounts of statistical data. This quantitative* approach to writing total history was advocated by members of the *Annales** school and was exemplified by the work of the historian Fernand Braudel.*

As Ginzburg himself recalls, in the years following the publication of *The Night Battles* "the paradigm that out of convenience I have called Braudelian was rapidly declining … [In] the course of the 1970s and 1980s the history of mentalities to which Braudel attributed a marginal significance acquired increasingly greater importance, often under the name of historical anthropology."[2]

The great interest *The Night Battles* elicited at the time of its publication can in many ways be attributed to the novel methods it introduced to the study of the history of mentalities.

Limitations

Carlo Ginzburg's *The Night Battles* was influential in the field of early-modern* history both for its aims and for its innovative methods. The work was also of interest to anthropologists, notably scholars of shamanism* and of comparative religion, for the account of shamanism it contained. As the social historian E. William Monter* notes, by "enormously extending the habitats of loosely related crypto-shamans both geographically and chronologically, Ginzburg has supplanted [the anthropologist] Mircea Eliade* as an obligatory reference for European historians who discuss shamans."[3]

Generally, the work received more criticism from specialists in the history of European witchcraft than it did from those outside the field. These critics have mostly targeted Ginzburg's tendency to draw large generalizations from limited and localized source materials. The witchcraft historian Norman Cohn,* for instance, pointed out that Ginzburg's argument for a pan-European agrarian cult was an over-generalization of his evidence.[4] As the historian Anthony Pagden* remarked, in a review of *The Night Battles* published in the *London Review of Books*, the "most obvious problem is to be found in the documents he has used. We know little about the daily lives of peasants for the simple reason that the so-called 'dominant culture' took very little interest in them."[5]

NOTES

1   István Szijártó, "Four Arguments for Microhistory," *Rethinking History* 6, no. 2 (2002): 209.

2   Carlo Ginzburg, "Microhistory: Two or Three Things That I Know About It," trans. John and Anne C. Tedeschi, *Critical Inquiry* 20, no. 1 (1993): 22.

3   E. William Monter, "Gendering the Extended Family of Ginzburg's
    Benandanti," *Magic, Ritual, and Witchcraft* 1, no. 2 (2006): 222.

4   Norman Cohn, "Book Review: The Night Battles," New Republic, February
    25, 1985.

5   Anthony Pagden, "Being a Benandante," *London Review of Books*, February
    2, 1984.

MODULE 8
PLACE IN THE AUTHOR'S WORK

KEY POINTS

- The major focus of Ginzburg's work has been on popular beliefs in the early-modern* period.

- A school of microhistory* developed as a result of Ginzburg's work in *The Night Battles*.

- Ginzburg's later work, *The Cheese and the Worms*, has arguably had even more influence than *The Night Battles* on the discipline of history.

Positioning

Published at the beginning of his academic career, *The Night Battles* was Carlo Ginzburg's first major-length work of history. He has since written several other books and numerous articles, and each of these has built upon the work he began in *The Night Battles*.

Although *The Night Battles* is an early work, it has a confidence and clarity usually associated with mature historians. Later developments in Ginzburg's work are clearly rooted in the same cross-disciplinary methods he developed here. His subsequent books include a highly influential examination of the mental world of an Italian tradesman, *The Cheese and the Worms: The Cosmos of a Sixteenth-Century Miller* (1976), and a study of the visionary traditions in early-modern* Europe, *Ecstasies: Deciphering the Witches' Sabbath* (1989).

Ginzburg also wrote several influential essays in which he developed and defended the methodology of microhistory.[1] As Ginzburg recalled in his essay "Microhistory,"[2] the school emerged gradually and became fully developed only after the publication of *The Night Battles*.

> ❝ In the early 1960s I began to study Inquisitorial trials in an attempt to reconstruct, in addition to the attitudes of the judges, those of the men and women accused of witchcraft ... [The] historiographical, conceptual and narrative implications of such a choice became clarified for me only gradually, in the course of the years that separated *The Night Battles* (1966) from *Ecstasies* (1989). ❞
>
> Carlo Ginzburg, "Microhistory: Two or Three Things That I Know About It"

Integration

The Night Battles can be seen as the germ out of which grew the school of microhistory.

Ginzburg's publications as a whole inspired a sub-genre of historical research and writing that the historian Brad Gregory* has called "episodic microhistory"—an approach that seeks to draw out through "relentless scrutiny of a specific encounter or a seemingly minor 'episode' ... aspects of a past society and culture that resist disclosure through more conventional historical methods."[3]

Ginzburg's methodological writings, collected in *Clues, Myths and the Historical Method* (1986), have had a significant impact on historical writing in the past two decades. The essays in this seminal work developed the idea that underlying realities could be better understood when historians acted like detectives who gather clues, rather than as compilers of quantitative* data. Ginzburg set out his method of "detective work" in a key article "Clues: Morelli, Freud and Sherlock Holmes,"[4] in which he suggested using specific, singular phenomena to illuminate broader structures.

Significance

Ginzburg's two most widely read and influential works are *The Night Battles* and *The Cheese and the Worms*. These two books back up his belief that poor and marginal figures from outside the elite can provide the basis for large-scale historical arguments. As the foundation for the intellectual school of microhistory itself, they have had a profound influence on the study and writing of history.

Following *The Night Battles,* Ginzburg published *Ecstasies,*[5] an exploration of European witch practices that developed the research he had begun in *The Night Battles.* Ginzburg's achievement in his first book is clearly apparent in this work's wide-ranging and field-shaping influence.

In the decades after the publication of *The Night Battles,* a number of works were published by historians following the microhistorical techniques developed by Ginzburg. Among these were Emmanuel Le Roy Ladurie's* *Montaillou* (1975), Natalie Zemon Davis's* *The Return of Martin Guerre* (1983), and Giovanni Levi's* *Inheriting Power* (1984).

However, Ginzburg's 1976 book *The Cheese and the Worms*—in which the methodological implications of his approach were more fully realized—was arguably even more influential in the development of microhistory than *The Night Battles.* As the Finnish historian Matti Peltonen has remarked, since the publication of these works "the flow of microhistories has been constant, though more variable in quality and without any really popular successes."[6]

NOTES

1 Carlo Ginzburg, *Clues, Myths, and the Historical Method*, trans. John and Anne C. Tedeschi (Baltimore, MD: Johns Hopkins University Press, 1989).

2 Carlo Ginzburg, "Microhistory: Two or Three Things That I Know About It," trans. John and Anne C. Tedeschi, *Critical Inquiry* 20, no. 1 (1993): 10–35.

3 Brad S. Gregory, "Is Small Beautiful? Microhistory and the History of Everyday Life," 101. *History and Theory* 38, no. 1 (1999): 102.

4 Carlo Ginzburg, "Clues: Morelli, Freud and Sherlock Holmes," in *The Sign of the Three: Dupin, Holmes, Pierce,* ed. Umberto Eco and Thomas A. Sebeok (Bloomington: Indiana University Press, 1988).

5   Carlo Ginzburg, *Ecstasies: Deciphering the Witches' Sabbath*, trans. Raymond Rosenthal (New York: Pantheon Books, 1991).

6   Matti Peltonen "Clues, Margins and Monads: The Micro–Macro Link in Historical Research," *History and Theory* 40, no. 3 (2001): 348.

SECTION 3
IMPACT

MODULE 9
THE FIRST RESPONSES

KEY POINTS

- *The Night Battles* was criticized for overgeneralizing from limited evidence.
- Carlo Ginzburg's work appeared at a time of heightened interest in the relationship between popular and elite culture in the early-modern* period.
- Ginzburg argued that conventional standards of historical evidence were not applicable to the history of popular culture.

Criticism

Soon after its translation into English, Carlo Ginzburg's *The Night Battles* was attacked by critics for its tendency to draw sweeping conclusions on the basis of a relatively limited number of sources.

Ginzburg was interested in discovering the hidden meanings in a set of sixteenth-century texts. Predictably perhaps, critics seized on his reliance on what was missing from the texts rather than on what they actually contained.[1] Others (the cultural historian* Roger Chartier,* for instance) saw Ginzburg's microscopic lens in a more positive light, concluding that "it is on this reduced scale, and probably only on this reduced scale, that we can understand, without deterministic* reduction, the relationships between systems of beliefs, of values and representations on the one hand, and social affiliations on the other."[2]

If Ginzburg's second book, *The Cheese and the Worms: The Cosmos of a Sixteenth-Century Miller*, drew more critical responses, those criticisms provided an opportunity for a more general critique of the microhistorical* approach developed in *The Night Battles*.

> **"**Reality is fundamentally discontinuous and heterogeneous. Consequently, no conclusion attained apropos a determinate sphere can be transferred automatically to a more general sphere. **"**
>
> Carlo Ginzburg, "Microhistory: Two or Three Things That I Know About It"

In a significant critique of Ginzburg's work, the Italian historian Paola Zambelli* argued that the popular beliefs Ginzburg had uncovered among peasants in the Friuli region were in fact derived from the elite culture of their own day—Aristotelianism,* a form of philosophy derived from the work of the Greek philosopher Aristotle.[3] Zambelli attacked the distinction Ginzburg had made between "elite" and "popular" culture, revealing these categories to be themselves modern constructions.

The literary scholar Dominick LaCapra* offered a similar critique of *The Cheese and the Worms*, jokingly arguing that the book in fact presented "The Cosmos of a Twentieth-Century Historian."[4]

Responses

Ginzburg responded to critics who accused him of relying on a historically groundless dichotomy—or a contrast between two things usually seen as being entirely different. He addressed this supposed dichotomy between popular and elite culture in a lengthy footnote to the 1980 edition of *The Cheese and the Worms*. While he did not reject the possibility of "circular, reciprocal or mutually-influential relations between elite and popular culture," he nevertheless maintained that the distinction between a predominantly oral popular culture and a written elite culture was important.[5]

Ginzburg also defended himself from the historian Anthony Pagden's* criticism of the "sometimes shaky nature of the arguments and assumptions" he developed in *The Night Battles*. In a response to

Pagden's review in the *London Review of Books*, Ginzburg argued that the stringent measures for evaluating evidence desired by Pagden were simply not possible in a study investigating the popular mentalities* of sixteenth-century peasants. "I can only wonder," he wrote, "if what separates me from Pagden is really a radical difference over what is commonly described as 'historical method.' I should at once add that this suspicion is mutual."[6]

Ginzburg would develop a systematic defense of the methods of microhistory in a number of important methodological articles that were published in the collection *Clues, Myths and the Historical Method*.

Conflict and Consensus

One of the key questions raised by *The Night Battles*, and by Ginzburg's work more generally, is the relationship between the part and the whole, the micro and the macro—what the historian Matti Peltonen has called the "Micro–Macro Link in Historical Research."[7] How truly representative is the evidence presented by microhistorians? How far can such "typical" evidence be used in the pursuit of historical explanation?

Ginzburg vigorously defended his method, while also conceding some of its limitations. The distinctive, singular qualities of the microhistorical approach, Ginzburg wrote, offer "both the greatest difficulty and the greatest potential benefits" to historical research. He defended attacks on the generalizable nature of his evidence by adopting a skeptical attitude toward historical truth in general, concluding that "reality is fundamentally discontinuous and heterogeneous ... no conclusion attained apropos a determinate sphere can be transferred automatically to a more a general sphere."[8]

Ultimately, Ginzburg argued that, as far evidence was concerned, fewer conventional standards simply had to be adopted if the history of the popular classes in early-modern Europe were ever to be written. Historians could only hope to write about what the cultural historian

Natalie Zemon Davis* called "the social creativity of the so-called inarticulate" if they accepted new standards of historical evidence adaptable to new kinds of history.[9]

NOTES

1   Alberto Tenenti, *Studi Storici* 8 (1967): 385–90.

2   Roger Chartier, "Intellectual History or Sociocultural history," in *Modern European Intellectual History: Reappraisals and New Perspectives*, ed. Dominick LaCapra and Steven L. Kaplan (Ithaca: Cornell University Press, 1982), 32.

3   Paola Zambelli, "From Menocchio to Piero Della Francesca: The Work of Carlo Ginzburg," *The Historical Journal* 28, no. 4 (1985).

4   Dominick LaCapra, "The Cheese and the Worms: The Cosmos of a Twentieth-Century Historian," in *History and Criticism* (Ithaca: Cornell University Press, 1985): 45– 70.

5   Carlo Ginzburg, *The Cheese and the Worms: The Cosmos of a Sixteenth-Century Miller*, trans. John and Anne C. Tedeschi (Baltimore, MD: Johns Hopkins University Press, 1980), 155.

6   Carlo Ginzburg, "Letter," *London Review of Books*, April 19, 1984.

7   Matti Peltonen "Clues, Margins and Monads: The Micro–Macro Link in Historical Research," *History and Theory* 40, no. 3 (2001).

8   Carlo Ginzburg, "Microhistory: Two or Three Things That I Know About It," trans. John and Anne C. Tedeschi, *Critical Inquiry* 20, no. 1 (1993): 27, 33.

9   Natalie Zemon Davis, *Society and Culture in Early Modern France: Eight Essays* (Stanford: Stanford University Press, 1975), 122.

MODULE 10
THE EVOLVING DEBATE

KEY POINTS

- Carlo Ginzburg's work significantly reduced the conventional parameters of space and time used by historians.

- Ginzburg's *The Night Battles* was a foundational text for the microhistorical* approach.

- Outside the discipline of history, Ginzburg's work has had the greatest impact on the literary movement known as New Historicism.*

Uses and Problems

Carlo Ginzburg's *The Night Battles* significantly reduced the conventional geographical and temporal scale of historical writing. Partly through Ginzburg's influence, social historians in the 1970s and 1980s moved away from the approach known as total history* (a method, associated with the French historical journal known as *Annales*,* which makes use of statistical data to study history) to investigate increasingly smaller targets, such as villages and individual social groups. Emmanuel Le Roy Ladurie's* *Montaillou* and Natalie Zemon Davis's* *The Return of Martin Guerre*, for instance, focused respectively on a small medieval hamlet and the remarkable life-story of a sixteenth-century soldier.

Part of this narrowing of focus included the reduction of historical research to the individual minds of historical actors. Since it is in part an analysis of the beliefs of a small group of individuals, *The Night Battles* is a prime example of this microscopic narrowing of historical research.

❝In what follows, I try to give four arguments for micro-oriented social history. I think that it has a clear advantage over macro-oriented traditional social history owing to its four characteristics: it is appealing to the general public, it is realistic, it conveys personal experience and whatever it has in its focus, the lines branching out from this reach very far.❞

István Szijártó, "Four Arguments for Microhistory"

The book also influenced the ways in which historians viewed religion. While works from around the same time as Ginzburg's, such as Keith Thomas's* *Religion and the Decline of Magic,* interpreted religion as serving a functional role in society, Ginzburg considered religious belief as a meaningful historical force. In Thomas's account, which came after Ginzburg's, religion was seen as a means of organizing political and personal events in the lives of those outside the elite. In *The Night Battles,* Ginzburg treated the beliefs and practices of the *benandanti** as vital parts of their world view. In this way, he laid the path for other seminal works of religious history that focus on the vitality of popular beliefs and practices in times of religious change and upheaval—the historian Eamon Duffy's* *The Stripping of the Altars* being a good example.

Schools of Thought

The Night Battles was one of the first illustrations of the microhistorical approach, and Ginzburg was a founding member of the school it represented. Along with the historians Carlo Poni,* Giovanni Levi,* and Edoardo Grendi, Ginzburg helped define microhistory as a coherent approach in several key methodological articles. Together, these scholars have pushed social historians* to try to understand historical change by analysis of social and cultural factors rather than through economic or political factors.

The popularity of microhistory in the 1970s and 1980s brought about a turn in social history, and greater attention was paid to recovering the historical roles and voices of history's marginalized individuals by means of a tightly focused reconstruction of their day-to-day lives. The cultural historian* Roger Chartier,* for instance, was partly inspired by Ginzburg's work to seek to recuperate "the illuminations of the illiterate, the experiences of wisdom, the wisdom of fools, the silence of the child."[1]

The Night Battles, and microhistory more generally, has served as a source of inspiration outside of the historical discipline itself. The impact was particularly notable on the school of New Historicism, an approach to literary criticism that seeks to find the meaning of texts in their original social and cultural location.

If the New Historicists, chief among them the literary theorist and critic Stephen Greenblatt,* are not proper descendants of Ginzburg, we may consider them fellow travelers. They maintain microhistory's concern with the everyday but are not held to the same standards of evidence. As literary critics, New Historicists are apt to speculate, imagine, or create the mindset and beliefs of their subjects in order to better understand the historical setting of a literary text.

In Current Scholarship

The assessments of the current vitality of microhistory are mixed. Some have proclaimed microhistory long dead, and argue that its influence reached its peak in the 1990s. Yet others, such as the social historians Sigurður Gylfi Magnússon * and István Szijártó,* have recently remarked that microhistory is still "clearly in the ascendant."[2] These authors argue that the influence of postmodernism*—a school of thought which questions the possibility of any "correct" reading of history and which advocates the close skeptical readings of historical documents—has contributed to the continued popularity of microhistory. "This is probably due to the fact that as postmodernism has, if not changed, at least modified the intellectual milieu, the use of history as a reading was significantly reinforced. Micro-investigations have come to the fore as several historians have moved towards satisfying this public demand."[3]

In a rebuttal to those who would declare microhistory dead or exhausted, István M. Szíjártó has written "Four Arguments for Microhistory," an article that attempts to explain the continuing popularity of microhistory in the twenty-first century. This is evidenced in the publication of such major works as Alf Ludtke's *The History of Everyday Life* (1995) and Jacques Revel's *Jeux d'Échelles: La micro-analyse à l'expérience.*

Szíjártó presents arguments for micro-oriented social history that give it "a clear advantage over macro-oriented traditional social history,"[4] among which are its greater appeal to the general public, its realism, and its ability to convey personal experience.

NOTES

1   Roger Chartier, "Michel de Certeau: History, or Knowledge of the Other," in *On the Edge of the Cliff: History, Language and Practices*, trans. Lydia G. Cochrane (Baltimore, MD: Johns Hopkins University Press, 1997), 46.

2   Sigurður Gylfi Magnússon and István M. Szíjártó, *What is Microhistory?* (London: Routledge, 2013), 69.

3   Magnússon and Szíjártó, *What is Microhistory?* 69.

4   István Szijártó, "Four Arguments for Microhistory," *Rethinking History* 6, no. 2 (2002): 209.

MODULE 11
IMPACT AND INFLUENCE TODAY

KEY POINTS

- *The Night Battles* remains a pioneering example of the microhistorical* approach.
- There has recently been a shift away from microhistory back toward a wider vision and what is now called "deep history."
- *The Night Battles* raises interesting questions about the relationship between shamanism* and witchcraft.

Position

In many ways, Carlo Ginzburg's *The Night Battles* has been overshadowed by his more popular book, *The Cheese and the Worms*— although both share much in terms of concept and method.

Indeed, it is the approach used by Ginzburg in *The Night Battles*, rather than the claims made in the text itself, that has had a significant impact on historical writing. While the existence of the pan-European fertility cult* that Ginzburg believed he had found in the countryside of north-eastern Italy remains open to debate, the tools of microhistory remain in use today. Along with Ginzburg's other works, *The Night Battles* holds a place at the forefront of cultural history,* and in many important ways has become part of the mainstream of history writing. The publication of a new edition of *The Night Battles* in 2013 is an indication of continuing interest in the text.

The book maintains its relevance for contemporary historians, having led many to a greater consideration of the everyday lives of marginalized historical people. The historian John Brewer,* for

> **❝** To a certain degree, we have all become microhistorians. The professional requirements of doing scholarly research require it. **❞**
>
> Paula Findlen, "The Two Cultures of Scholarship"

example, has recently cited *The Night Battles* as a pioneering work of "history from below," in that it inspired "a large body of historical writing in the last forty years [to make] everyday life, the experiences, actions and habits of ordinary people a legitimate object of historical inquiry."[1]

Interaction

Since the 1960s, the historical profession has been gradually divided between what the historian Paula Findlen* has called the "two cultures of scholarship": the "microhistorical" and "the generalist vision." Findlen cites Ginzburg as a pioneer of the first approach, which advocates "that a close reading of singular episodes producing unusually rich documentation, preferably of people whose voices might otherwise go unheard, revealed a different and more complex understanding of the past." The second approach, the "generalist vision," has gone into significant decline due to the rising popularity of the methods of microhistory. As Findlen notes, "To a certain degree, we have all become microhistorians. The professional requirements of doing scholarly research require it."[2]

Yet critics of the microhistorical approach claim that the accumulation of microhistorical studies has made it hard to construct a new big picture from this mass of intimate detail. The increasingly microscopic level of research, critics argue, has come at the cost of creating a coherent narrative out of the past.[3]

The recent interest elicited by historian Daniel Smail's* essay, "On the Possibilities for a Deep History of Humankind,"[4] can be seen as part of a growing disillusionment with the approach advocated by Ginzburg. Deep history, as Smail writes, calls for a radical chronological and geographical expansion of the parameters currently used by historians. In many ways, the current interest aroused by the concept of deep history perhaps suggests a swing back to the vision of total history,* with its grand societal and structural focus, that Ginzburg helped displace.

The Continuing Debate

Ginzburg's *The Night Battles* serves as a key text in the debate over whether European witchcraft was descended from shamanism. The focus of this debate might be described by the question "How do the conclusions of *The Night Battles* both relate to and inform our understandings of the development and history of European witchcraft?"

It is a debate that includes questions about the relationship between witchcraft and shamanism—a suite of beliefs and rituals that usually center on the ability of ritual specialists to enter altered states of consciousness and to interact with good and evil forces "in the world of the spirit," usually for the good of the community to which the shaman belongs.

While Ginzburg does not use the word "shaman," the central figures in his story, the *benandanti*,* claimed to be bringing about good results, and a key point of *The Night Battles* was to argue that shamanistic practices extended from Asia into Western Europe. It is to this particular point that scholars of shamanism are attracted. The Dutch anthropologist Jeroen W. Boekhoven* has recently noted in *Genealogies of Shamanism* that *The Night Battles* continues to provoke debate within the field, deeming the work "impressive and admirable," but also with "shortcomings that cannot be ignored."[5]

NOTES

1   John Brewer, "Microhistory and the Histories of Everyday Life," *Cultural and Social History* 7, no. 1 (2010): 90.

2   Paula Findlen, "The Two Cultures of Scholarship?" *Isis* 96, no. 2 (2005): 234.

3   James A. Secord, "The Big Picture," *British Journal for the History of Science* 26 (1993): 387–483.

4   Daniel Smail, "On The Possibilities for a Deep History of Humankind," in *Emerging Disciplines: Shaping New Fields of Scholarly Inquiry In and Beyond the Humanities*, ed. Melissa Bailar (Houston: Rice University Press, 2010), 9–24.

5   Jeroen W. Boekhoven, *Genealogies of Shamanism: Struggles for Power, Charisma and Authority* (Groningen: Barkhuis, 2011), 9.

MODULE 12
WHERE NEXT?

KEY POINTS

- The critical approach to archival sources used by Carlo Ginzburg in *The Night Battles* continues to influence the practice of historical research.

- The microhistorical* approach developed in *The Night Battles* has recently come under competition from the more geographically expansive approach of global history.*

- *The Night Battles* remains a seminal text in the field of microhistory.

Potential

Carlo Ginzburg's *The Night Battles* will continue to be an important text. If his thesis is correct, and there was indeed a pan-European fertility cult* with origins in ancient Eurasia, then historians of ancient, medieval,* and early-modern* Europe have much to consider and many new avenues of research to follow. In any event, Ginzburg has made a considerable impact by provoking historians to reflect more critically on the nature of the sources and archives they use.

In recent decades, historians partly inspired by Ginzburg's work have coined the term "archival turn" to refer to the more critical approach to sources and archives taken in the past decades.[1] As the historian Shannon McSheffrey* has written, in an article that draws direct inspiration from Ginzburg's microhistorical approach, the crucial methodological question facing contemporary historians is "how can thinking about the archives as historical agents rather than as inert repositories of evidence refine the way we use historical documents?"[2]

> **"** Are the questions that propelled Italian microhistory still significant or have they lost their impetus? ... [And] what can this approach contribute nowadays, when 'globalization' and 'global' are the dominant keywords in the humanities and social sciences—key words that we hardly associate with anything micro? **"**
>
> Francesca Trivalleto, "Is There a Future for Italian Microhistory in the Age of Global History?"

The nature and appropriate use of sources is territory that has long been of interest to historians, and it is unlikely that debates over sources will end in the foreseeable future. The methodological approach developed in *The Night Battles*—which uses close readings of archival sources to shed light on the broader patterns of daily life in the past—continues to have a strong influence on social historians of the early-modern period.

Future Directions

Aside from the implications of its methodological innovations, *The Night Battles* will remain a seminal text in the field of religious studies for its pioneering analysis of the social meaning of popular religious beliefs within historical study. Avoiding functionalist* interpretations of religion (that is, avoiding the assumption that expressions of culture serve some identifiable and useful "purpose"), Ginzburg insisted the *benandanti*'s* religious beliefs ought to be treated as meaningful in their own right.

In this way, Ginzburg paved the way for other seminal works of religious history that focus on the vitality of popular practice and belief in times of religious change and upheaval, such as Eamon Duffy's* *The Stripping of the Altars*. Indeed, the past two decades have seen a boom in the study of lay practitioners and their beliefs. The "new religious history," a genre that uses methods drawn from the field of anthropology to study the religious beliefs and practices of the past, can be seen as a successor to Ginzburg's work.

As for the future of microhistory in general, historians have recently begun to wonder if its approach is still relevant as the turn toward global history continues to expand the historian's geographical horizons. Indeed, many advocates of global history have termed their approach macrohistory* in an act of self-conscious differentiation from microhistory.[3] Other historians have worked to combine the methods of global history and microhistory, maintaining that "the issues raised by Italian microhistorians may nonetheless provide constructive input for academic practitioners of global history."[4]

Summary

Carlo Ginzburg's *The Night Battles* well deserves the attention it has received. It is a text that has challenged the disciplinary expectations of history while both questioning and affirming several schools of historical research and analysis—the traditional Marxist* approach among them. Although Ginzburg's politics were influenced by Marxism, he challenged the Marxist historians' methodological focus on masses of people by centering his inquiry on individuals or small groups, such as the *benandanti*.

Through his analysis of the ways in which individuals made choices both within social structures and at their margins, Ginzburg also challenged the structuralist* idea that an individual's life is determined by a society's configurations. Moreover, he analyzed the persistence of certain religious practices after Christianity replaced the social structures that originally gave rise to them.

The impact of *The Night Battles* is bound up in the originality and unique nature of its ideas—and these ideas remain important because they stand as the basis for the school of thought called "microhistory."

The impact of the work permeates scholarship and thought in the field of history. Here, Ginzburg is considered a thinker and writer with a central position in the long-standing debate on the importance of the individual to history and to the structure of society alike.

As a work of early-modern history, *The Night Battles* is an investigation of the everyday beliefs of common rural folk who lived under certain religious, political, and economic structures. Many of Ginzburg's contemporaries focused their gaze on larger structures and, in doing so, overlooked Ginzburg's sources entirely. If Ginzburg's thesis is right—that there was a pan-European fertility cult existing from ancient times right through to the 1600s—then an important part of European history has been overlooked. Both Ginzburg's method and his subject matter act as potential criticisms of his contemporaries.

Ginzburg's claim that his sources could be explained by a pan-European cult observed by farming people ignored the perceived religious and cultural barriers between Europe and Asia. For some, this has changed what we must understand by the term "European history," and so sets the text apart from other works. Instead of thinking of Europe in geographical or political terms, Ginzburg considered how it related to the ideas and beliefs of people. As a result, the geographic scope of his inquiry is not confined to conceptions of European and Asian borders. Rather, his geographic space might better be described as a sphere in which an ancient, shamanistic* cult once thrived and persisted into the seventeenth century. This idea was an original contribution to historical scholarship on witchcraft, a field which typically relied on the terms of political and religious authority—on the categories, in other words, set up by the medieval and early-modern Roman Catholic Church.*

Ginzburg's work is further set apart by its treatment of the everyday beliefs of the less powerful and marginalized as a subject for meaningful historical inquiry. Rather than treat politics as the place to begin all analysis, and religion as politics by another name, Ginzburg allowed his politically marginal figures to express their own religious terms. In doing so, he put forward the view that popular beliefs—religious or otherwise—had significance in their own right.

By focusing on everyday beliefs rather than on larger structures such as politics and economics, Ginzburg conjured a story of early-modern and medieval European religion and society that was very different from the histories written by his contemporaries.

As a work of microhistory, *The Night Battles* takes the view that the study of history is the study of social inequality. Historical meaning arises from the tension between the socially and economically privileged and those excluded from that privilege, the divide between urban and rural living, and the minds of the learned and unlearned.

With these points in mind, the text's strong contribution to the study of popular culture is evident.

NOTES

1   See for instance: Arlette Farge, *Le Goût de l'archive* (Paris: Seuil, 1997).

2   Shannon McSheffrey, "Detective Fiction in the Archives: Court Records and the Uses of Law in Late Medieval England," *History Workshop Journal* 65 (2008): 65.

3   Donald A. Yerxa, "Introduction: History on a Large Scale," in *Recent Themes in World History and the History of the West: Historians in Conversation*, ed. Donald A. Yerxa (Columbia: South Carolina, 2009): 1–12.

4   Francesca Trivellato, "Is There a Future for Italian Microhistory in the Age of Global History?", *California Italian Studies* 2, no. 1 (2011): 20.

GLOSSARY

GLOSSARY OF TERMS

Annales **school:** named after the French academic journal *Annales d'Histoire Economique et Sociale* (Annals of Economic and Social History), which began publication in 1929. *Annales* historians aimed at the creation of "total history"—an approach that encompassed the social, mental, and economic past. Their work is seen as reforming the compartmentalized historical research of nineteenth-century France.

Anthropology: the scientific study of human beings and culture.

Aristotelianism: a tradition of philosophy that takes its defining inspiration from the work of Aristotle.

Benandanti: a loosely affiliated peasant group in rural northern Italy of the sixteenth and seventeenth centuries. Speakers of a regional dialect called Friulian, the *benandanti*—or "good walkers"— claimed they left their bodies at night in order to protect their crops by battling evil spirits.

Christianity: a major religion based on the life and teachings of Jesus Christ in the first century C.E.

Communism: a political and economic doctrine that rejects private ownership, and advocates that all property should be vested in the community for the benefit of all.

Cultural history: a branch of study that takes up the task of explaining the historical development of culture.

Determinism: a belief that social and cultural forms are fundamentally determined by the modes of economic production.

Early-modern period: the period of history following the Middle Ages and preceding the modern era. Although the exact dates of this period are a matter of debate, it is often accepted to have lasted from approximately 1500 to 1800.

Ethnocentric: a way of looking at things from the perspective of your own culture, and the belief that this is better or more important than other cultures and perspectives.

Fascism: a radical political ideology that privileges the unity and power of a nation or race over the flourishing of the individual by means of a centralized, authoritarian state that aims to suppress all opposition. It came to prominence in Europe in the 1920s and 1930s in such nations as Germany and Italy.

Fertility cult: a pagan tradition among agricultural peoples where rituals are enacted each year with the primary intention of making sure the approaching harvest is plentiful.

Functionalism: an approach in the social sciences that sees all social phenomena as tending toward the creation of stability and solidarity.

Global history: refers to the study of historical events that transcend national borders. Rather than the study of history confined to a specific nation state or society, global history is concerned with topics such as migration, environmental change, and the effects of encounters between civilizations and cultures.

Heresy/heretical: teachings or practices that are not endorsed by religious officials.

Historical anthropology: a field of historical research in which methods drawn from the field of anthropology are applied to the study of people from the past.

History of mentalities: the historical study of the mind (roughly, the attitudes, ideas, and assumptions) of people from the past.

Industrial capitalism: a form of economic organization based on the production of manufactured goods.

Industrialization: the process whereby a society transforms itself from an agricultural system into one based on the production of goods and services.

Inquisition: a body set up by the Roman Catholic Church to investigate heresy. Both the investigative methods and punishments were harsh, and included torture and death. The Inquisition began in the twelfth century, operated intermittently, and ended in the nineteenth century.

Intellectual left: refers to intellectuals who are broadly wedded to politics of social equality and egalitarianism.

Jew: members of the Jewish faith, Judaism. Judaism is a religion believing in one God that originated in the Middle East and that traces its beginnings back 3,000 years. Christianity emerged from one of the many different Jewish movements that existed in the first century C.E.

Macrohistory: refers to the method of historical analysis that examines historical change over big timescales and geographical areas and for large numbers of people. Historians following this method frequently look for similarities between events separated by periods of time and geographical distance in order to identify hypothetical patterns and structures.

Marxism: a theory that claims historical change occurs through class conflict and transformations in the economic means of production.

Medieval period: also known as the Middle Ages, a period in European history that lasted from the fifth to the fifteenth centuries.

Microhistory: the close analysis of everyday sources. Microhistory was developed as a response to grand narrative histories that diminished or ignored the historical role of the individual. Carlo Ginzburg was one of the founders of this method.

Microsocial: in the field of sociology, microsocial refers to small-scale interactions that take place between particular individuals—that is, face to face.

New Historicism: a movement that sought to apply the tools of historical research to uncovering the meaning of texts.

Postmodernism: in historical studies postmodernism assumes there are no grand narratives and therefore no final "meanings" to be found. Rather, all historical meaning is localized to the individual person. A key figure is the theoretician Jean-François Lyotard (1924–98), whose works include *Phenomenology* (1998).

Quantitative history: the practice of making claims about the past based on the accumulation of statistical data.

Reformation: The Reformation was a schism within Western Christianity that lasted, roughly, from 1517 to 1648 and saw the founding of the Protestant tradition.

Roman Catholic Church: the largest and oldest of the Christian denominations. The head of the Roman Catholic Church is the Pope, who resides in the Vatican in Italy. Approximately half of all Christians worldwide are Roman Catholics.

Serial history: a historical methodology that seeks to establish patterns in the past through the analysis of large quantities of statistical data.

Shamanism: a suite of beliefs and rituals that center on the ability of ritual specialists to enter altered states of consciousness and to intercede with good and evil forces, usually for the good of the community to which they belong.

Social history: a field of history that examines the dynamics of social groups rather than individuals.

Sociology: the academic study of the structures, history, and processes that define societies.

Structural-functionalist: an alternative term for "functionalist"—an approach in the social sciences that sees all social phenomena as tending toward the creation of stability and solidarity.

Structuralism: a method of analysis that relates expressions of culture to larger, overarching social structures.

Structural sociology: a scholarly view that culture must be considered in the light of larger structures that define societies—particularly economics and class.

Total history: an effort to write the economic, political, social, and cultural history of a people or region. It is often identified with the *Annales* school of historians.

Vatican: a walled enclave within the city of Rome that acts as the principal seat of the Roman Catholic Church.

Witch hunt: a term used for the hunting out of people believed to be witches or for evidence of the practice of witchcraft, often stoked by a sense of moral outrage and general hysteria. Witch hunts took place in Europe in the early-modern period, and as many as 100,000 people were killed.

Witches' sabbath: in the late medieval era, the witches' sabbath was considered the central cultic practice of witchcraft. It involved the inversion and perversion of Roman Catholic symbols, dancing, nudity, and kissing images of the devil.

World War II: a global conflict between 1939 and 1945 that pitted the Axis powers of Nazi Germany, fascist Italy, and imperial Japan against the Allied nations, including Britain, the USA, and the USSR.

PEOPLE MENTIONED IN THE TEXT

Mikhail Mikhailovich Bakhtin (1895–1975) was a Russian philosopher and literary theorist. He is noted for his work in the philosophy of language and for his role in the early development of the theory of signs and symbols, or "semiotics."

David A. Bell (b. 1964) is a professor of history at Princeton University.

Walter Benjamin (1892–1940) was a German philosopher and cultural critic whose work on daily life in nineteenth-century Paris has become an important text for contemporary urban anthropologists.

Marc Bloch (1886–1944) was a French historian who wrote *The Royal Touch: Sacred Monarchy and Scrofula in England and France.* Bloch was a founding member of the *Annales* school of history.

Jeroen W. Boekhoven (b. 1963) is a Dutch sociologist and anthropologist.

Fernand Braudel (1902–85) was a French historian who had substantial influence over historical writing in the West. He focused on geographically (rather than politically) defined units and analyzed long-term social and economic changes rather than events or individuals. See, especially, *The Mediterranean and the Mediterranean World in the Age of Philip II.*

John Brewer (b. 1947) is a historian of eighteenth-century Britain.

Delio Cantimori (1904–66) was an Italian historian of the Protestant Reformation.

Roger Chartier (b. 1945) is a cultural historian of early-modern France.

Norman Cohn (1915–2007) was a historian of religion and witchcraft.

Natalie Zemon Davis (b. 1928) is a cultural historian of early-modern France.

Eamon Duffy (b. 1947) is an Irish historian and a professor at Cambridge University.

Mircea Eliade (1907–86) was an influential Romanian anthropologist, religious historian, and author, noted for his work in myth and shamanism.

E. E. Evans-Pritchard (1902–73) was an English anthropologist who helped found the discipline of social anthropology.

Lucien Febvre (1878–1956) was a French historian and founding member of the *Annales* school.

Paula Findlen (b. 1964) is a historian of science at Stanford University.

François Furet (1927–97) was a French historian of the French Revolution and a political philosopher.

Clifford Geertz (1926–2006) was an American anthropologist. His significant works include *Myth, Symbol, Culture* (1971) and *The Interpretation of Cultures* (1973).

Leone Ginzburg (1909–44) was Carlo Ginzburg's father, a professor of Russian literature in Pisa, Italy, and a specialist on the Russian intellectual Mikhail Bakhtin.

Natalia Ginzburg (1916–91) was Carlo Ginzburg's mother and an Italian novelist.

Stephen Greenblatt (b. 1943) is an American literary critic and professor of the humanities at Harvard University.

Brad Gregory (b. 1963) is a professor of history at Notre Dame University.

Siegfried Kracauer (1889–1966) was a German philosopher.

Dominick LaCapra (b. 1939) is a professor of history at Cornell University.

Emmanuel Le Roy Ladurie (b. 1929) is a French historian, noted for his pioneering work in early-modern French popular culture.

Giovanni Levi (b. 1939) is a historian and founding member of the Italian microhistory school.

Claude Lévi-Strauss (1908–2009) was a French anthropologist and ethnologist who developed a theory called "structuralism" which interpreted culture by relating it to larger social structures.

Alan Macfarlane (b. 1941) is an anthropologist and historian, and a professor at Cambridge University.

Shannon McSheffrey is a professor in the History Department at Concordia University in Montreal, Quebec. A historian of later medieval and early Tudor England, her particular research interests are gender roles, law, civic culture, marriage, literacy, heresy, and popular religion.

E. William Monter (b. 1936) is a social historian of early-modern Europe.

Sigurður Gylfi Magnússon (b. 1957) is an Icelandic social historian.

Benito Mussolini (1883–1945) was the leader of the National Fascist Party in Italy and the country's leader from 1922 to 1943.

Anthony Pagden (b. 1945) is a historian of early-modern Europe.

Carlo Poni (b. 1927) is a historian, and a founding member of the Italian microhistory school.

Vladimir Propp (1895–1970) was a Russian scholar who studied the forms of myths of different cultures and developed a comparative methodology called "formalism."

Georg Simmel (1858–1918) was a German sociologist whose pioneering works on daily life in the city make him a precursor of urban sociology.

Daniel Smail (b. 1967) is a medieval historian at Harvard University.

István Szijártó (b. 1965) is a Hungarian social historian.

Keith Thomas (b. 1933) is a noted Welsh-born cultural historian of early-modern Britain, and former professor of History at Oxford University.

E. P. Thompson (1924–93) was a British Marxist historian known primarily for his 1963 work, *The Making of the English Working Class.*

Hugh Trevor-Roper (1914–2003) was a British historian who worked on a wide range of subjects, including Adolf Hitler and early-modern European religion.

Paola Zambelli (b. 1936) is an Italian historian of early-modern witchcraft and magic.

WORKS CITED

WORKS CITED

Anglo, Sydney, ed. *The Damned Art: Essays in the Literature of Witchcraft.* London, Henley, and Boston: Routledge & Kegan Paul, 1977.

Ariès, Philippe. "L'Histoire des mentalités." In *La Nouvelle Histoire,* edited by Jacques Legoff, Roger Chartier, and Jacques Revel, 396–425. Paris: Retz-CEPL, 1978.

Bednarski, Steven. *A Poisoned Past: The Life and Times of Margarida De Portu, A Fourteenth-Century Accused Poisoner.* Toronto: University of Toronto Press, 2014.

Bell, David A. "Total History and Microhistory: The French and Italian Paradigms." In *A Companion to Western Historical Thought*, edited by Lloyd Kramer and Sarah Maza, 262–76. Oxford: Blackwell, 2002.

Boekhoven, Jeroen W. *Genealogies of Shamanism: Struggles for Power, Charisma and Authority.* Groningen: Barkhuis, 2011.

Braudel, Fernand. *The Mediterranean and the Mediterranean World in the Age of Philip II.* New York: Harper and Row, 1972.

Brewer, John. "Microhistory and the Histories of Everyday Life." *Cultural and Social History* 7 (2010): 87–109.

Burke, Peter. *The French Historical Revolution: The Annales School, 1929–1989.* Cambridge: Polity Press, 1990.

Chartier, Roger. "Intellectual History or Sociocultural history." In *Modern European Intellectual History: Reappraisals and New Perspectives,* edited by Dominick LaCapra and Steven L. Kaplan, 13–47. Ithaca: Cornell University Press, 1982.

"Michel de Certeau: History, or Knowledge of the Other." In *On the Edge of the Cliff: History, Language and Practices.* Translated by Lydia G. Cochrane. Baltimore, MD: Johns Hopkins University Press, 1997.

Cohn, Norman. "Book Review: The Night Battles." *The New Republic*, February 25, 1985.

Collins, James B., and Karen L. Taylor. *Early Modern Europe: Issues and Interpretations*. Oxford: Blackwell, 2006.

Davidson, Arnold I. *The Emergence of Sexuality: Historical Epistemology and the Formation of Concepts.* Cambridge, MA: Harvard University Press, 2001.

Davis, Natalie Zemon. *Society and Culture in Early Modern France: Eight Essays.* Stanford: Stanford University Press, 1975.

Farge, Arlette. *Le Goût de l'archive.* Paris: Seuil, 1997.

Findlen, Paula. "The Two Cultures of Scholarship?" *Isis* 96, no.2 (2005): 230–7.

Furay, Conal, and Michael J. Salevouris. *The Methods and Skills of History: A Practical Guide.* Oxford: Wiley & Sons, 2015.

Gaskill, Malcolm. "The Pursuit of Reality: Recent Research into the History of Witchcraft." *The Historical Journal* 51, no. 4 (2008): 1069–88.

Ginzburg, Carlo. *The Cheese and the Worms: The Cosmos of a Sixteenth-Century Miller.* Translated by John and Anne C. Tedeschi. Baltimore, MD: Johns Hopkins University Press, 1980.

"Clues: Morelli, Freud and Sherlock Holmes." In *The Sign of the Three: Dupin, Holmes, Pierce,* edited by Umberto Eco and Thomas A. Sebeok. Bloomington: Indiana University Press, 1988.

Clues, Myths, and the Historical Method. Translated by John and Anne C. Tedeschi. Baltimore, MD: Johns Hopkins University Press, 1989.

Ecstasies: Deciphering the Witches' Sabbath. Translated by Raymond Rosenthal. New York: Pantheon Books, 1991.

"Letter," *London Review of Books*, April 19, 1984.

"Microhistory: Two or Three Things That I Know About It." Translated by John and Anne C. Tedeschi. *Critical Inquiry* 20, no. 1 (1993): 10–35.

The Night Battles: Witchcraft and Agrarian Cults in the Sixteenth and Seventeenth Centuries. Translated by John and Anne C. Tedeschi. Baltimore, MD: Johns Hopkins University Press, 2013.

Ginzburg, Carlo, and Carlo Poni. "The Name and the Game: Unequal Exchange and the Historiographic Marketplace." In *Microhistory and the Lost Peoples of Europe*, edited by Edward Muir and Guido Ruggiero, 1–10. Baltimore, MD: Johns Hopkins University Press, 1991.

Giswijt-Hofstra, Marijke. "The European Witchcraft Debate and the Dutch Variant." *Social History* 15, no. 2 (1990): 181–94.

Gregory, Brad S. "Is Small Beautiful? Microhistory and the History of Everyday Life." *History and Theory* 38, no. 1 (1999): 100–10.

LaCapra, Dominick. "The Cheese and the Worms: The Cosmos of a Twentieth-Century Historian." In *History and Criticism,* 45–70. Ithaca: Cornell University Press, 1985.

Macfarlane, Alan. *Witchcraft in Tudor and Stuart England: A Regional and Comparative Study.* London: Routledge, 1970.

Magnússon, Sigurður Gylfi, and István M. Szíjártó. *What is Microhistory?* London: Routledge, 2013.

Martin, John. "Journey to the World of the Dead: The Work of Carlo Ginzburg." *Journal of Social History* 25, no. 3 (1992): 613–26.

McSheffrey, Shannon. "Detective Fiction in the Archives: Court Records and the Uses of Law in Late Medieval England." *History Workshop Journal* 65 (2008): 65–78.

Monter, E. William. "Gendering the Extended Family of Ginzburg's Benandanti." *Magic, Ritual, and Witchcraft* 1, no. 2 (2006): 222–6.

"The Historiography of European Witchcraft: Progress and Prospects." *Journal of Interdisciplinary History* 2, no. 4 (1972): 435–53.

Muir, Edward, and Guido Ruggiero, eds. *Microhistory and the Lost Peoples of Europe*. Baltimore, MD: Johns Hopkins University Press, 1991

Pagden, Anthony. "Being a Benandante." *London Review of Books*, February 2, 1984.

Peltonen, Matti. "Clues, Margins and Monads: The Micro–Macro Link in Historical Research." *History and Theory* 40, no. 3 (2001): 348.

Secord, James A. "The Big Picture," *British Journal for the History of Science* 26 (1993): 387–483.

Smail, Daniel. "On The Possibilities for a Deep History of Humankind." In *Emerging Disciplines: Shaping New Fields of Scholarly Inquiry in and beyond the Humanities*, edited by Melissa Bailar, 9–24. Houston: Rice University Press, 2010.

Szijártó, István. "Four Arguments for Microhistory." *Rethinking History* 6, no. 2 (2002): 209–15.

Tenenti, Alberto. *Studi Storici* 8 (1967): 385–90.

Thomas, Keith. "The Relevance of Social Anthropology to the Historical Study of English Witchcraft." In *Witchcraft Confessions and Accusations*, edited by Mary Douglas, 47–80. London: Routledge Library Editions, 1970.

Religion and the Decline of Magic. New York: C. Scribner's Sons, 1971.

Thompson, E. P. *The Making of the English Working Class*. London: Victor Gollancz, 1963.

Trevor-Roper, H. R. *Religion, the Reformation, and Social Change*. 2nd edn. London: Macmillan, 1972.

Trivellato, Francesca. "Is There a Future for Italian Microhistory in the Age of Global History?" *California Italian Studies* 2, no. 1 (2011): 1–26.

Yerxa, Donald A. "Introduction: History on a Large Scale." In *Recent Themes in World History and the History of the West: Historians in Conversation,* edited by Donald A. Yerxa, 1–12. Columbia: University of South Carolina Press, 2009.

Zambelli, Paola. "From Menocchio to Piero Della Francesca: The Work of Carlo Ginzburg." *The Historical Journal* 28, no. 4 (1985): 983–99.

THE MACAT LIBRARY
BY DISCIPLINE

AFRICANA STUDIES

Chinua Achebe's *An Image of Africa: Racism in Conrad's Heart of Darkness*
W. E. B. Du Bois's *The Souls of Black Folk*
Zora Neale Huston's *Characteristics of Negro Expression*
Martin Luther King Jr's *Why We Can't Wait*
Toni Morrison's *Playing in the Dark: Whiteness in the American Literary Imagination*

ANTHROPOLOGY

Arjun Appadurai's *Modernity at Large: Cultural Dimensions of Globalisation*
Philippe Ariès's *Centuries of Childhood*
Franz Boas's *Race, Language and Culture*
Kim Chan & Renée Mauborgne's *Blue Ocean Strategy*
Jared Diamond's *Guns, Germs & Steel: the Fate of Human Societies*
Jared Diamond's *Collapse: How Societies Choose to Fail or Survive*
E. E. Evans-Pritchard's *Witchcraft, Oracles and Magic Among the Azande*
James Ferguson's *The Anti-Politics Machine*
Clifford Geertz's *The Interpretation of Cultures*
David Graeber's *Debt: the First 5000 Years*
Karen Ho's *Liquidated: An Ethnography of Wall Street*
Geert Hofstede's *Culture's Consequences: Comparing Values, Behaviors, Institutes and Organizations across Nations*
Claude Lévi-Strauss's *Structural Anthropology*
Jay Macleod's *Ain't No Makin' It: Aspirations and Attainment in a Low-Income Neighborhood*
Saba Mahmood's *The Politics of Piety: The Islamic Revival and the Feminist Subject*
Marcel Mauss's *The Gift*

BUSINESS

Jean Lave & Etienne Wenger's *Situated Learning*
Theodore Levitt's *Marketing Myopia*
Burton G. Malkiel's *A Random Walk Down Wall Street*
Douglas McGregor's *The Human Side of Enterprise*
Michael Porter's *Competitive Strategy: Creating and Sustaining Superior Performance*
John Kotter's *Leading Change*
C. K. Prahalad & Gary Hamel's *The Core Competence of the Corporation*

CRIMINOLOGY

Michelle Alexander's *The New Jim Crow: Mass Incarceration in the Age of Colorblindness*
Michael R. Gottfredson & Travis Hirschi's *A General Theory of Crime*
Richard Herrnstein & Charles A. Murray's *The Bell Curve: Intelligence and Class Structure in American Life*
Elizabeth Loftus's *Eyewitness Testimony*
Jay Macleod's *Ain't No Makin' It: Aspirations and Attainment in a Low-Income Neighborhood*
Philip Zimbardo's *The Lucifer Effect*

ECONOMICS

Janet Abu-Lughod's *Before European Hegemony*
Ha-Joon Chang's *Kicking Away the Ladder*
David Brion Davis's *The Problem of Slavery in the Age of Revolution*
Milton Friedman's *The Role of Monetary Policy*
Milton Friedman's *Capitalism and Freedom*
David Graeber's *Debt: the First 5000 Years*
Friedrich Hayek's *The Road to Serfdom*
Karen Ho's *Liquidated: An Ethnography of Wall Street*

The Macat Library By Discipline

John Maynard Keynes's *The General Theory of Employment, Interest and Money*
Charles P. Kindleberger's *Manias, Panics and Crashes*
Robert Lucas's *Why Doesn't Capital Flow from Rich to Poor Countries?*
Burton G. Malkiel's *A Random Walk Down Wall Street*
Thomas Robert Malthus's *An Essay on the Principle of Population*
Karl Marx's *Capital*
Thomas Piketty's *Capital in the Twenty-First Century*
Amartya Sen's *Development as Freedom*
Adam Smith's *The Wealth of Nations*
Nassim Nicholas Taleb's *The Black Swan: The Impact of the Highly Improbable*
Amos Tversky's & Daniel Kahneman's *Judgment under Uncertainty: Heuristics and Biases*
Mahbub Ul Haq's *Reflections on Human Development*
Max Weber's *The Protestant Ethic and the Spirit of Capitalism*

FEMINISM AND GENDER STUDIES

Judith Butler's *Gender Trouble*
Simone De Beauvoir's *The Second Sex*
Michel Foucault's *History of Sexuality*
Betty Friedan's *The Feminine Mystique*
Saba Mahmood's *The Politics of Piety: The Islamic Revival and the Feminist Subject*
Joan Wallach Scott's *Gender and the Politics of History*
Mary Wollstonecraft's *A Vindication of the Rights of Woman*
Virginia Woolf's *A Room of One's Own*

GEOGRAPHY

The Brundtland Report's *Our Common Future*
Rachel Carson's *Silent Spring*
Charles Darwin's *On the Origin of Species*
James Ferguson's *The Anti-Politics Machine*
Jane Jacobs's *The Death and Life of Great American Cities*
James Lovelock's *Gaia: A New Look at Life on Earth*
Amartya Sen's *Development as Freedom*
Mathis Wackernagel & William Rees's *Our Ecological Footprint*

HISTORY

Janet Abu-Lughod's *Before European Hegemony*
Benedict Anderson's *Imagined Communities*
Bernard Bailyn's *The Ideological Origins of the American Revolution*
Hanna Batatu's *The Old Social Classes And The Revolutionary Movements Of Iraq*
Christopher Browning's *Ordinary Men: Reserve Police Batallion 101 and the Final Solution in Poland*
Edmund Burke's *Reflections on the Revolution in France*
William Cronon's *Nature's Metropolis: Chicago And The Great West*
Alfred W. Crosby's *The Columbian Exchange*
Hamid Dabashi's *Iran: A People Interrupted*
David Brion Davis's *The Problem of Slavery in the Age of Revolution*
Nathalie Zemon Davis's *The Return of Martin Guerre*
Jared Diamond's *Guns, Germs & Steel: the Fate of Human Societies*
Frank Dikotter's *Mao's Great Famine*
John W Dower's *War Without Mercy: Race And Power In The Pacific War*
W. E. B. Du Bois's *The Souls of Black Folk*
Richard J. Evans's *In Defence of History*
Lucien Febvre's *The Problem of Unbelief in the 16th Century*
Sheila Fitzpatrick's *Everyday Stalinism*

Eric Foner's *Reconstruction: America's Unfinished Revolution, 1863-1877*
Michel Foucault's *Discipline and Punish*
Michel Foucault's *History of Sexuality*
Francis Fukuyama's *The End of History and the Last Man*
John Lewis Gaddis's *We Now Know: Rethinking Cold War History*
Ernest Gellner's *Nations and Nationalism*
Eugene Genovese's *Roll, Jordan, Roll: The World the Slaves Made*
Carlo Ginzburg's *The Night Battles*
Daniel Goldhagen's *Hitler's Willing Executioners*
Jack Goldstone's *Revolution and Rebellion in the Early Modern World*
Antonio Gramsci's *The Prison Notebooks*
Alexander Hamilton, John Jay & James Madison's *The Federalist Papers*
Christopher Hill's *The World Turned Upside Down*
Carole Hillenbrand's *The Crusades: Islamic Perspectives*
Thomas Hobbes's *Leviathan*
Eric Hobsbawm's *The Age Of Revolution*
John A. Hobson's *Imperialism: A Study*
Albert Hourani's *History of the Arab Peoples*
Samuel P. Huntington's *The Clash of Civilizations and the Remaking of World Order*
C. L. R. James's *The Black Jacobins*
Tony Judt's *Postwar: A History of Europe Since 1945*
Ernst Kantorowicz's *The King's Two Bodies: A Study in Medieval Political Theology*
Paul Kennedy's *The Rise and Fall of the Great Powers*
Ian Kershaw's *The "Hitler Myth": Image and Reality in the Third Reich*
John Maynard Keynes's *The General Theory of Employment, Interest and Money*
Charles P. Kindleberger's *Manias, Panics and Crashes*
Martin Luther King Jr's *Why We Can't Wait*
Henry Kissinger's *World Order: Reflections on the Character of Nations and the Course of History*
Thomas Kuhn's *The Structure of Scientific Revolutions*
Georges Lefebvre's *The Coming of the French Revolution*
John Locke's *Two Treatises of Government*
Niccolò Machiavelli's *The Prince*
Thomas Robert Malthus's *An Essay on the Principle of Population*
Mahmood Mamdani's *Citizen and Subject: Contemporary Africa And The Legacy Of Late Colonialism*
Karl Marx's *Capital*
Stanley Milgram's *Obedience to Authority*
John Stuart Mill's *On Liberty*
Thomas Paine's *Common Sense*
Thomas Paine's *Rights of Man*
Geoffrey Parker's *Global Crisis: War, Climate Change and Catastrophe in the Seventeenth Century*
Jonathan Riley-Smith's *The First Crusade and the Idea of Crusading*
Jean-Jacques Rousseau's *The Social Contract*
Joan Wallach Scott's *Gender and the Politics of History*
Theda Skocpol's *States and Social Revolutions*
Adam Smith's *The Wealth of Nations*
Timothy Snyder's *Bloodlands: Europe Between Hitler and Stalin*
Sun Tzu's *The Art of War*
Keith Thomas's *Religion and the Decline of Magic*
Thucydides's *The History of the Peloponnesian War*
Frederick Jackson Turner's *The Significance of the Frontier in American History*
Odd Arne Westad's *The Global Cold War: Third World Interventions And The Making Of Our Times*

LITERATURE

Chinua Achebe's *An Image of Africa: Racism in Conrad's Heart of Darkness*
Roland Barthes's *Mythologies*
Homi K. Bhabha's *The Location of Culture*
Judith Butler's *Gender Trouble*
Simone De Beauvoir's *The Second Sex*
Ferdinand De Saussure's *Course in General Linguistics*
T. S. Eliot's *The Sacred Wood: Essays on Poetry and Criticism*
Zora Neale Huston's *Characteristics of Negro Expression*
Toni Morrison's *Playing in the Dark: Whiteness in the American Literary Imagination*
Edward Said's *Orientalism*
Gayatri Chakravorty Spivak's *Can the Subaltern Speak?*
Mary Wollstonecraft's *A Vindication of the Rights of Women*
Virginia Woolf's *A Room of One's Own*

PHILOSOPHY

Elizabeth Anscombe's *Modern Moral Philosophy*
Hannah Arendt's *The Human Condition*
Aristotle's *Metaphysics*
Aristotle's *Nicomachean Ethics*
Edmund Gettier's *Is Justified True Belief Knowledge?*
Georg Wilhelm Friedrich Hegel's *Phenomenology of Spirit*
David Hume's *Dialogues Concerning Natural Religion*
David Hume's *The Enquiry for Human Understanding*
Immanuel Kant's *Religion within the Boundaries of Mere Reason*
Immanuel Kant's *Critique of Pure Reason*
Søren Kierkegaard's *The Sickness Unto Death*
Søren Kierkegaard's *Fear and Trembling*
C. S. Lewis's *The Abolition of Man*
Alasdair MacIntyre's *After Virtue*
Marcus Aurelius's *Meditations*
Friedrich Nietzsche's *On the Genealogy of Morality*
Friedrich Nietzsche's *Beyond Good and Evil*
Plato's *Republic*
Plato's *Symposium*
Jean-Jacques Rousseau's *The Social Contract*
Gilbert Ryle's *The Concept of Mind*
Baruch Spinoza's *Ethics*
Sun Tzu's *The Art of War*
Ludwig Wittgenstein's *Philosophical Investigations*

POLITICS

Benedict Anderson's *Imagined Communities*
Aristotle's *Politics*
Bernard Bailyn's *The Ideological Origins of the American Revolution*
Edmund Burke's *Reflections on the Revolution in France*
John C. Calhoun's *A Disquisition on Government*
Ha-Joon Chang's *Kicking Away the Ladder*
Hamid Dabashi's *Iran: A People Interrupted*
Hamid Dabashi's *Theology of Discontent: The Ideological Foundation of the Islamic Revolution in Iran*
Robert Dahl's *Democracy and its Critics*
Robert Dahl's *Who Governs?*
David Brion Davis's *The Problem of Slavery in the Age of Revolution*

Alexis De Tocqueville's *Democracy in America*
James Ferguson's *The Anti-Politics Machine*
Frank Dikotter's *Mao's Great Famine*
Sheila Fitzpatrick's *Everyday Stalinism*
Eric Foner's *Reconstruction: America's Unfinished Revolution, 1863-1877*
Milton Friedman's *Capitalism and Freedom*
Francis Fukuyama's *The End of History and the Last Man*
John Lewis Gaddis's *We Now Know: Rethinking Cold War History*
Ernest Gellner's *Nations and Nationalism*
David Graeber's *Debt: the First 5000 Years*
Antonio Gramsci's *The Prison Notebooks*
Alexander Hamilton, John Jay & James Madison's *The Federalist Papers*
Friedrich Hayek's *The Road to Serfdom*
Christopher Hill's *The World Turned Upside Down*
Thomas Hobbes's *Leviathan*
John A. Hobson's *Imperialism: A Study*
Samuel P. Huntington's *The Clash of Civilizations and the Remaking of World Order*
Tony Judt's *Postwar: A History of Europe Since 1945*
David C. Kang's *China Rising: Peace, Power and Order in East Asia*
Paul Kennedy's *The Rise and Fall of Great Powers*
Robert Keohane's *After Hegemony*
Martin Luther King Jr.'s *Why We Can't Wait*
Henry Kissinger's *World Order: Reflections on the Character of Nations and the Course of History*
John Locke's *Two Treatises of Government*
Niccolò Machiavelli's *The Prince*
Thomas Robert Malthus's *An Essay on the Principle of Population*
Mahmood Mamdani's *Citizen and Subject: Contemporary Africa And The Legacy Of Late Colonialism*
Karl Marx's *Capital*
John Stuart Mill's *On Liberty*
John Stuart Mill's *Utilitarianism*
Hans Morgenthau's *Politics Among Nations*
Thomas Paine's *Common Sense*
Thomas Paine's *Rights of Man*
Thomas Piketty's *Capital in the Twenty-First Century*
Robert D. Putman's *Bowling Alone*
John Rawls's *Theory of Justice*
Jean-Jacques Rousseau's *The Social Contract*
Theda Skocpol's *States and Social Revolutions*
Adam Smith's *The Wealth of Nations*
Sun Tzu's *The Art of War*
Henry David Thoreau's *Civil Disobedience*
Thucydides's *The History of the Peloponnesian War*
Kenneth Waltz's *Theory of International Politics*
Max Weber's *Politics as a Vocation*
Odd Arne Westad's *The Global Cold War: Third World Interventions And The Making Of Our Times*

POSTCOLONIAL STUDIES

Roland Barthes's *Mythologies*
Frantz Fanon's *Black Skin, White Masks*
Homi K. Bhabha's *The Location of Culture*
Gustavo Gutiérrez's *A Theology of Liberation*
Edward Said's *Orientalism*
Gayatri Chakravorty Spivak's *Can the Subaltern Speak?*

The Macat Library By Discipline

PSYCHOLOGY

Gordon Allport's *The Nature of Prejudice*
Alan Baddeley & Graham Hitch's *Aggression: A Social Learning Analysis*
Albert Bandura's *Aggression: A Social Learning Analysis*
Leon Festinger's *A Theory of Cognitive Dissonance*
Sigmund Freud's *The Interpretation of Dreams*
Betty Friedan's *The Feminine Mystique*
Michael R. Gottfredson & Travis Hirschi's *A General Theory of Crime*
Eric Hoffer's *The True Believer: Thoughts on the Nature of Mass Movements*
William James's *Principles of Psychology*
Elizabeth Loftus's *Eyewitness Testimony*
A. H. Maslow's *A Theory of Human Motivation*
Stanley Milgram's *Obedience to Authority*
Steven Pinker's *The Better Angels of Our Nature*
Oliver Sacks's *The Man Who Mistook His Wife For a Hat*
Richard Thaler & Cass Sunstein's *Nudge: Improving Decisions About Health, Wealth and Happiness*
Amos Tversky's *Judgment under Uncertainty: Heuristics and Biases*
Philip Zimbardo's *The Lucifer Effect*

SCIENCE

Rachel Carson's *Silent Spring*
William Cronon's *Nature's Metropolis: Chicago And The Great West*
Alfred W. Crosby's *The Columbian Exchange*
Charles Darwin's *On the Origin of Species*
Richard Dawkin's *The Selfish Gene*
Thomas Kuhn's *The Structure of Scientific Revolutions*
Geoffrey Parker's *Global Crisis: War, Climate Change and Catastrophe in the Seventeenth Century*
Mathis Wackernagel & William Rees's *Our Ecological Footprint*

SOCIOLOGY

Michelle Alexander's *The New Jim Crow: Mass Incarceration in the Age of Colorblindness*
Gordon Allport's *The Nature of Prejudice*
Albert Bandura's *Aggression: A Social Learning Analysis*
Hanna Batatu's *The Old Social Classes And The Revolutionary Movements Of Iraq*
Ha-Joon Chang's *Kicking Away the Ladder*
W. E. B. Du Bois's *The Souls of Black Folk*
Émile Durkheim's *On Suicide*
Frantz Fanon's *Black Skin, White Masks*
Frantz Fanon's *The Wretched of the Earth*
Eric Foner's *Reconstruction: America's Unfinished Revolution, 1863-1877*
Eugene Genovese's *Roll, Jordan, Roll: The World the Slaves Made*
Jack Goldstone's *Revolution and Rebellion in the Early Modern World*
Antonio Gramsci's *The Prison Notebooks*
Richard Herrnstein & Charles A Murray's *The Bell Curve: Intelligence and Class Structure in American Life*
Eric Hoffer's *The True Believer: Thoughts on the Nature of Mass Movements*
Jane Jacobs's *The Death and Life of Great American Cities*
Robert Lucas's *Why Doesn't Capital Flow from Rich to Poor Countries?*
Jay Macleod's *Ain't No Makin' It: Aspirations and Attainment in a Low Income Neighborhood*
Elaine May's *Homeward Bound: American Families in the Cold War Era*
Douglas McGregor's *The Human Side of Enterprise*
C. Wright Mills's *The Sociological Imagination*

Thomas Piketty's *Capital in the Twenty-First Century*
Robert D. Putman's *Bowling Alone*
David Riesman's *The Lonely Crowd: A Study of the Changing American Character*
Edward Said's *Orientalism*
Joan Wallach Scott's *Gender and the Politics of History*
Theda Skocpol's *States and Social Revolutions*
Max Weber's *The Protestant Ethic and the Spirit of Capitalism*

THEOLOGY

Augustine's *Confessions*
Benedict's *Rule of St Benedict*
Gustavo Gutiérrez's *A Theology of Liberation*
Carole Hillenbrand's *The Crusades: Islamic Perspectives*
David Hume's *Dialogues Concerning Natural Religion*
Immanuel Kant's *Religion within the Boundaries of Mere Reason*
Ernst Kantorowicz's *The King's Two Bodies: A Study in Medieval Political Theology*
Søren Kierkegaard's *The Sickness Unto Death*
C. S. Lewis's *The Abolition of Man*
Saba Mahmood's *The Politics of Piety: The Islamic Revival and the Feminist Subject*
Baruch Spinoza's *Ethics*
Keith Thomas's *Religion and the Decline of Magic*

COMING SOON

Chris Argyris's *The Individual and the Organisation*
Seyla Benhabib's *The Rights of Others*
Walter Benjamin's *The Work Of Art in the Age of Mechanical Reproduction*
John Berger's *Ways of Seeing*
Pierre Bourdieu's *Outline of a Theory of Practice*
Mary Douglas's *Purity and Danger*
Roland Dworkin's *Taking Rights Seriously*
James G. March's *Exploration and Exploitation in Organisational Learning*
Ikujiro Nonaka's *A Dynamic Theory of Organizational Knowledge Creation*
Griselda Pollock's *Vision and Difference*
Amartya Sen's *Inequality Re-Examined*
Susan Sontag's *On Photography*
Yasser Tabbaa's *The Transformation of Islamic Art*
Ludwig von Mises's *Theory of Money and Credit*

Macat Pairs

*Analyse historical and modern issues
from opposite sides of an argument.
Pairs include:*

Macat Pairs

Analyse historical and modern issues from opposite sides of an argument. Pairs include:

HOW WE RELATE TO EACH OTHER AND SOCIETY

Jean-Jacques Rousseau's
The Social Contract

Rousseau's famous work sets out the radical concept of the 'social contract': a give-and-take relationship between individual freedom and social order.

If people are free to do as they like, governed only by their own sense of justice, they are also vulnerable to chaos and violence. To avoid this, Rousseau proposes, they should agree to give up some freedom to benefit from the protection of social and political organization. But this deal is only just if societies are led by the collective needs and desires of the people, and able to control the private interests of individuals. For Rousseau, the only legitimate form of government is rule by the people.

Robert D. Putnam's
Bowling Alone

In *Bowling Alone*, Robert Putnam argues that Americans have become disconnected from one another and from the institutions of their common life, and investigates the consequences of this change.

Looking at a range of indicators, from membership in formal organizations to the number of invitations being extended to informal dinner parties, Putnam demonstrates that Americans are interacting less and creating less "social capital" – with potentially disastrous implications for their society.

It would be difficult to overstate the impact of *Bowling Alone*, one of the most frequently cited social science publications of the last half-century.

Printed in the United States
by Baker & Taylor Publisher Services